WISDOM, INC.

Seth Godin

HarperBusiness
A Division of HarperCollins*Publishers*

HarperCollins books may be purchased for educational, business, or sales pro-
motional use. For information please write: Special Markets Department,
HarperCollins Publishers, Inc., 10 East 53rd Street, New York, NY 10022.

FIRST EDITION

Designed by Karen Engelmann

ISBN 0-88730-758-2

95 96 97 98 99   RRD   10 9 8 7 6 5 4 3 2 1

For Alexander, Joel, Flynn, Alessandra, Matthew, and Cooper

ACKNOWLEDGMENTS

At least a dozen people worked hard to create *Wisdom, Inc.* Project manager Robin Dellabough researched, edited, wrote, oversaw the survey process, and interviewed respondents. Lisa DiMona was instrumental in getting the project up and running. Karen Watts, Julie Maner, Amy Winger, and Jen Gniady contributed mightily—commenting and kibitzing as the book developed.

Thanks also to the rest of the extraordinary SGP staff, Carol Markowitz, Megan O'Connor, Anthony Schneider, Dan Lovy, and Lucy Wood. Every day they proved that the advice in this book really works. And bouquets of wheat to Karen Engelmann for her design flair.

The core of the book was our national survey, for which we are grateful for the exceptional support of helpful people at two organizations: John F. Raynolds, Bill Robertson, and Sam Marks at Ward Howell International Inc., and Michael Winkleman and Bristol Lane Voss at *The Journal of Business Strategy*.

A special thanks to Melissa Birritella, Chris Cory, Mitzi Sales, Skye Hallberg, Bruce Blackburn, and Kevin Dolan.

Finally, thanks to Adrian Zackheim and Suzanne Oaks, our line editors at HarperCollins.

My parents, teachers, friends, and my wife, Helene, have helped me realize that the more you put into life, the more you get out of living. I hope that some of their insight comes through to you.

Contact us at: Box 321, Dobbs Ferry, NY 10522. (914) 693-7711, or e-mail: seth@yoyo.com

CONTENTS

Foreword...vii

Preface..ix

Introduction..1

Copy of the Actual Survey 7

Attention to Detail...9

Balanced Lifestyle 15

Creativity...19

Curiosity..26

Drive..31

Efficiency..35

Ethics 40

Fearlessness...46

Focus 51

Goals...56

Grace Under Pressure..61

Hard Work...66

Initiative..71

Integrity 76

Intelligence...82

Leadership 87

Loyalty 93

Persistence...98

Resourcefulness...103

Responsibility...108

Self-motivation 113

Sense of Humor..118

Sense of Ownership 123

Strategy 129

Teamwork 134

Vision..140

Notes 145

FOREWORD

In this book, Seth Godin has literally written "something for everyone." That sounds fairly presumptuous for a foreword, but he has compiled information which will be invaluable to anyone serious about being, doing and having the good things in life. I firmly believe that you've got to be before you can do, and you must do before you can have.

The research Seth has done on the values, qualities and attributes which are considered critical for success by people who are successful is impressive. He has identified qualities that will be helpful, whether an individual is a household executive, a college professor, salesperson, member of the military, physician, coach, or simply "good old Joe," trying to make the best of life.

Outstanding executives around the country have decreed that ethics, teamwork, honesty, curiosity, hard work, intelligence, self-motivation and a sense of humor all are important. These qualities, when developed and applied, will help anyone acquire more of the things money will buy and all of the things money won't buy.

Here is a book that will be helpful to you. The book is easy reading and virtually every page contains usable information. Those who apply the message daily in their personal and family life, as well as in their career, will benefit enormously. You will want to read it, and keep it handy for reference. *Wisdom, Inc.* is a major contribution toward achieving balanced success.

Zig Ziglar

PREFACE

When I was twelve, my father taught me how to ski.

The first few lessons were pretty easy. I had absurdly short skis, and I quickly learned how to do parallel turns and traverse.

Then I plateaued. I could ski but not very well. I'd lean back and head down the slope but I felt all the excitement of riding a bicycle.

"Lean forward," my dad would say.

Leaning forward struck me as a ridiculous concept. I was already going down a steep hill—actually, more like a mountain. Leaning forward seemed like a maneuver that would surely lead to hurtling over a cliff and definite serious injury.

After a few weeks of fighting my dad's advice, I happened to catch some ski racing on "Wide World of Sports." "These guys really know how to ski," I said to myself. "How do they do it?" I watched carefully, and soon learned the trick: they all leaned forward.

Turns out that leaning forward is the secret of skiing. When you lean forward, you commit to the slope. Instead of coasting, you carve your turns on the mountain. The stakes get higher—the decisions that you make each second become crucial. You are more fully engaged with the sport and with yourself.

Unfortunately, most skiers never learn to lean forward. Leaning back is easier, simpler, safer. It's more natural. But it leads to mediocre skiing.

I haven't skied in a while, but working on this book made me think a lot about that early lesson. Because this is a book about leaning forward. It's about how to change your attitude at work in a way that your bosses, co-workers, and employees will notice and appreciate.

That may sound simple. It is. But there's absolutely nothing easy about changing attitudes. Just as I resisted my father's "simple" instruction to lean forward, you're likely to let fear and inertia keep you from changing your approach to work.

It doesn't have to be that way. Stop for a minute. Look around your workplace. Find the people who are engaged, happy, motivated. Aren't they also the ones getting the best projects, the fastest promotions, the most job security? Chances are, they're leaning forward.

Nearly every business book written in the last twenty years identifies attitude as a crucial element in a company's success. When employees are engaged, committed and motivated, a company's profit, market share, and long term growth potential go off the charts.

Something else happens as well. Employees' lives are changed.

A long time ago, I decided that life's too short to waste even one day sleepwalking through a deadend job, checking your watch, and waiting for the next coffee break or the end of the day or for the weekend. This book is your wake-up call. Make a commitment to adopting the virtues and attitudes outlined in the following pages. Try it for thirty days.

If you do, you'll enjoy your job more. You'll enjoy your family more. You'll have more energy. You'll be leaning forward, racing down the ski slope of life, feeling fully alive. Your life will change. Mine did.

Send me e-mail and let me know how the book helped you. Meanwhile, I'll see you on the mountain!

Seth Godin
Dobbs Ferry, New York
seth@yoyo.com

INTRODUCTION

Imagine for a minute that you own a really first-class restaurant. You and your investors have spent more than $800,000, to lease and renovate a space, train the staff, and advertise. You've been open three months and business is still a little slow.

At five o'clock one Saturday a good friend of yours, who works at the city paper, calls. In hushed tones, he says he just heard that the paper's restaurant critic is dining at your restaurant tonight. Incognito of course. A bad review could wipe you out; four stars could mean a full house for years.

So what would you do? What would you tell your waiters and waitresses, your maitre d', your chef? How would you want people to behave, the food to look, the restaurant to feel?

Now, here's a better question: Wouldn't you want it to be that way *every* night?

You can bet that on this particular Saturday night every member of your restaurant staff is on his/her toes waiting for the restaurant critic to arrive. But once the pressure's off, once the boss looks the other way, most people have a natural tendency to coast a little.

This book is the result of a survey we sent to more than 20,000 mid-level and top managers around the country, asking them, in essence, what would keep that restaurant staff performing as if a critic was in the house every night—whether or not the boss was there. What qualities would they seek and encourage in employees and in themselves to help their companies succeed? What separates an exceptional employee from a mediocre one? What are the most important business virtues?

THE SURVEY

Exactly one survey respondent, a business owner from South Dakota, checked *well-groomed* as an important virtue. The same person was one of only six who checked *punctual*. Not a single soul said *humble*, but then people who look for *humble* probably aren't humble themselves. Read on for further tidbits culled from the hundreds of questionnaires we received.

Our quest for virtues began with the help of the leading executive recruiting firm, Ward Howell International, Inc. Chairman John Raynolds sent out 8,000 letters to top business executives nationwide. He asked them to fill out the one-page survey reprinted on page 7.

In addition, the *Journal of Business Strategy*, a magazine with a circulation of 15,000, ran a full-page survey for readers to tear out and return.

We didn't know what to expect. We had no preconceived agenda. As the responses came in via fax and mail, it wasn't only their sheer volume that impressed us. It soon became clear that we had created a lightning rod for a discussion of values in the workplace. People were very eager to share their ideas on the subject of business virtues. We were stunned by the thought and time shown by the answers, considering the hectic schedules most of these executives maintain. When busy executives take time out to fill in a survey, it must be because they are genuinely intrigued with the subject. Many wrote variations on the theme of "This is a great idea" or "I can't wait to read this book" or "A much needed book." Others picked up the phone to find out more about the project. Still others agreed to talk with us in depth about their answers.

One enthusiastic respondent even brought the survey to his church in Greenwich, Connecticut. The minister there made it the focus of an ongoing weekly discussion group. Soon church members were debating the difference between *ethical* and *responsible*, both in their personal and in their work lives.

From IBM to NBC, from Alcoa to Colgate-Palmolive, some of America's top corporations are represented in this survey. We heard from those in most major industries, including financial services, communications, consumer products, health care, education, and manufacturing. In terms of management levels, there were 181 vice presidents, 176 presidents, 90 directors, and 67 CEOs or COOs, for a total of 524 out of about 700 respondents.

Plenty of small business owners and entrepreneurs were interested in virtues as well. In fact, we could almost guess which category respondents represented from simply glancing at their answers. The buttoned-down types tended to stress ethical, honest, and teamwork oriented. Their entrepreneurial counterparts liked curious, creative, and proactive.

Although responses came from every state, we didn't find any particular geographic weighting toward one virtue over another. For example, if stereotypes are to be believed, we might assume that Californians would check *balanced lifestyle* more often than New Yorkers. They didn't. New York must be catching up (or vice versa). The survey contained absolutely no geographical clichés at all.

When we ranked virtues by percentage the top ten turned out to be:

49% Ethics
38% Teamwork
36% Honesty
35% Curiosity
27% Hard work
26% Intelligence
22% Self-motivation
16% Sense of humor
16% Initiative
15% Creativity

Regardless of the virtues chosen, our respondents were passionate in their responses. Over and over we read identical descriptions of different virtues: "Without this virtue, all others are meaningless," or "This virtue encompasses all the others," or "You can teach everything else but this virtue." Apparently, executives are certain that their virtues are the best virtues.

To some extent, such variation is semantic. If you take a look at the original survey list of virtues, it's easy to see that many of them are similar, if not synonymous. One person's *hardworking* is another's *productive*. Or, as the song goes, you say visionary, I say conceptual, you say *persistent*, I say *tenacious*. In a few cases, we combined responses that we thought truly had identical meanings—instead of poetic license, call it survey prerogative. We realize there are always subtle denotations, but trust our respondents won't mind if we interpreted *attention to detail* to mean *thorough*.

The semantic issue comes up again in looking at what people filled in under *other*—almost every one could be considered the same as one of the virtues we did list: effective, experimental, caring, analytical, adaptable, dependable, efficient, trustworthy, good communicator, entrepreneurial, customer focused, flexible, positive, knows to ask for help.

Our personal favorites, however, were: *horse sense* and *lucky*. We should all be so...

TOWARD VIRTUOSITY

The book is organized around twenty-six virtues, each described in anecdotes, quotes, statistics, and examples. Included for many virtues are summaries of our survey findings for that particular virtue. Each chapter concludes with a "Toward Virtuosity" section in which we suggest a few concrete ways to practice and strengthen the virtue. We purposely kept these tips and exercises low-key, gentle, and open-ended. We think you'll find them both effective and fun.

There's no need to read straight through from beginning to end. This book rewards the browser equally richly. We suggest you start by looking over the reprinted survey and listing your own top ten most important virtues. Then look up each one and see how others rate them and apply them.

Or pick the three traits you think you need to develop and use the practical steps toward mastery. If you could do a much better job if you were in on brainstorming meetings, volunteer for the next one. If you're nuts about people being organized, it's important that you share that data.

Can you measure these virtues? Why not? It's not as easy as computing how many widgets are assembled per hour, but it's not that tough either. The Toward Virtuosity section contains ways to benchmark your virtues. So you can use this book as a reference for giving and receiving job performance feedback.

We take for granted that people know they should be thorough and quality conscious and self-motivated. The truth is:

These virtues aren't easy habits. If they were, we'd already be practicing them. Business virtues are learned skills. They require effort and lots of feedback and praise in order to flourish. Most employees need a road map, a specific list of what to concentrate on. Such a blueprint of exactly what will make the most impact is rarely offered to a new—or even an older—employee.

But consider: what if your workplace were populated by bosses who encourage employees to go the extra mile for a client, who—for example—reward a cashier for running after a customer who left a twenty-dollar bill when he meant to leave a five? What if America were filled with employees like the Federal Express driver who rented a helicopter to fly over a blocked road to deliver a package? Or the taxi driver in New York who offers passengers magazines to read while they travel?

All you need—all anyone needs—is a book of business virtues. So here it is, a handbook for getting hooked on the satisfaction and thrill of good work…better work…the *best* work.

☺ *The Book of Business Virtues:* Survey*

Next year, HarperCollins, publishers of *Reengineering the Corporation* and *In Search of Excellence*, will publish *The Book of Business Virtues*. This is the first book that attempts to codify the important habits, attitudes and skills that employers look for in an employee.

We need your help in order to make our survey as accurate as possible. The thoughts, insights and contributions of survey respondents will make the book more effective. Will you take a minute to answer these two questions and fax us back your response?

1. Of these 'virtues,' which five are the most important to you in employees and co-workers? *(Please circle five.)*

Always Learning	Fearless	Organized	Sincere
Attention to Detail	Focused	Patient	Stamina
Balanced Lifestyle	Generous	Perceptive	Strategic
Challengeable	Goal Oriented	Persistent	Teamwork Oriented
Conceptual	Good Self Esteem	Personable	Tenacious
Conscientious	Grace Under Pressure	Proactive	Thorough
Consistent	Hard Working	Productive	Time Aware
Creative	Honest	Punctual	Visionary
Curious	Humble	Resourceful	Well Groomed
Driven	Independent	Respected	Willing to Take the Blame
Empathetic	Intelligent	Responsible	Willing to Dream
Energetic	Knows to Ask for Help	Self Motivated	Other_____
Engaged	Leader	Sense of Humor	
Ethical	Loyal	Sense of Ownership	

2. Please choose one virtue and tell us *why* you think it's important to your company.

_____

_____

_____

Share your thoughts with us:
If you have stories, anecdotes or ideas about the role of virtues in the workplace, we'd love to hear from you. Please attach them to this survey.

Attach your business card here or type below:

Your name_____

Title_____

Company_____

Address_____

City_____ State_____ Zip_____

Phone_____ FAX_____

FAX YOUR RESPONSE BY DECEMBER 15.

Please return to Seth Godin Productions. Fax: (914) 693-8132. Mail: Box 660, Dobbs Ferry, NY 10522. Feel free to call us at (914) 693-7711.

*Note: The title on the original survey, *The Book of Business Virtues*, was subsequently changed to *Wisdom, Inc.*

Attention to
DETAIL

A white tablecloth with one tiny ink
spot on it is more than 99 percent clean. But
every person who sees it will remember the
stain, not the rest of the cloth.

*D*etails can build empires. Walt Disney's huge business was made, in large part, by how much attention he paid to details. From creating tiny cartoon images to flying over Disneyland twice a week to spot-check for cleanliness, Disney knew that if enough details were perfect, the end product would be too.

Disney's approach has stuck. At most other amusement parks, the streets get cleaned at night. The average life expectancy of a piece of gum discarded on Main Street at Disney World is less than fifteen minutes. Little details add up to more than just a clean park. They reflect an attitude that pervades the organization.

For the Opticon Company, a three-cent earplug translated into a tremendous increase in new business. The hearing-aid company was getting requests from customers, mostly audiologists, for free replacement parts. After the chief financial officer revealed that an earplug cost the company only three cents, management decided to send people *five* free earplugs every time they asked for just one. Not only did the new policy attract new business, many customers who had previously dropped Opticon came back. A three-cent earplug isn't a big deal. Until you need one and can't find it. Because of such attention to detail, according to company president Peter Hahn, monthly customer calls went up from 4,000 to 10,000 within six months.

There's an accountant at Fidelity who has worked hard all his life. He stayed late, kept his nose to the grindstone, and moved up the organization. Then, when working on a spreadsheet that computed the annual return of the Magellan Fund, the largest mutual fund in the world, he failed to recheck his numbers. The result: Magellan reported a profit instead of a loss.

When the mistake was found, it generated international headlines. All the hard work, all the late nights, don't mean anything because of one missed detail. For the rest of his career, the accountant will be known as the guy who made the mistake on the Magellan Fund.

Rick Johnson, founder and CEO of BurJon Steel Service Center Inc., thinks there's more to life than money. When his employees have to work overtime, he sends flowers and coupons for dinner at a local restaurant, often directly to the employee's spouse, along with a personal note. "When somebody works hard, it's hard on everyone," he says. "We think it's important to say thanks."

The flowers themselves aren't as important as the fact that the CEO took the time to send them. As soon as he delegates the task to an assistant, they'll mean a lot less.

Harvey Mackay has built a $50 million business by paying attention to details. The Mackay Envelope Company sales force keeps detailed lists about each client's life—birthdays, family events, favorite chocolate bar, etc. You can bet that every single one of his customers gets a personal birthday card every year. That's a lot of attention from a little envelope company— but that translates into attention to quality as well.

When Benjamin Franklin solicited printing work from the Pennsylvania state government he discovered it was in the hands of Andrew Bradford, a competitor whose work was notoriously sloppy. So Franklin got his hands on a copy of a speech the governor had made, reprinted it on fancy paper in elegant type—without a single typographical error—and sent it to the governor and to each member of the assembly. The legislators, impressed by Franklin's attention to detail, soon awarded him all the state's printing business.

Lack of attention to detail can result in tragedy. The space shuttle *Challenger* exploded because a fifteen-cent rubber part did not function in unusually cold weather. Several brilliant scientists were killed and a multibillion-dollar program was jeopardized because this one tiny detail was overlooked.

"It has long been an axiom of mine that the little things are infinitely the most important." Sherlock Holmes

---

An old hand in training seminars for American Airlines always used the following example to explain the critical importance of details: *Every day thousands of employees worked incredibly hard to ensure a passenger's loyalty to American Airlines. But if a reservation was wrong, or the ticket was written out incorrectly, or the flight got out late, or the crew wasn't friendly, or the bag was missing, it didn't matter to the passenger that everything else was perfect. One mistake by one employee could mean that the work of thousands—from the corporate office to the maintenance hangars to the cockpit crew—had gone for naught.*

Have you ever received a cover letter from a job applicant that read, "I am responding to your ad in the *New Times*"? Or, worse yet, your own name was misspelled? How likely were you to follow up on this person? It's a fact of life that typos can reflect a general lack of attention to detail—which in turn seems to spell out to all of us a lack of quality.

In *Quality Is Free*, Philip Crosby wrote that it's better to build in quality than to inspect for quality. In almost every situation, the cost of building something right in the first place is a small fraction of the cost of having an inspector catch mistakes and then fix them.

What you said about
ATTENTION TO DETAIL

As a financial planning organization, we customize our recommendations to meet the needs of our clients. Lack of attention to detail would be our undoing.

BARBARA SUTTON
Chief Financial Officer, The Acacia Group

As a provider of financial information and an intermediary between our clients and investors, it is vital that everything we produce, distribute, and/or say be factually correct and appear crisp, organized, and neat.

JOHN HIGGINS
Broadgate Consultants

TOWARD VIRTUOSITY

Do the people you most admire have a habit of being thorough? Ask them how they do it.

Sometimes you can spend too much time on one kind of detail when others are much more crucial. Know when details *don't* count. Make a list of the details that are important in your job.

Choose one detail from your list, whether it's checking spelling or stock returns, and concentrate on it for a week.

Don't underestimate the value of checklists. Pilots work their way through more than one hundred items before their jets are cleared for takeoff. Can you create a checklist for the items that leave your desk or workplace?

Tom Peters is really clear on this point: "If you measure it, it gets done." Does your company have small benchmarks you can measure yourself against? Does your staff know what they are?

Balanced
LIFESTYLE

A balanced lifestyle doesn't
necessarily mean less work and more play.
It does involve caring for yourself on every
level: your body, your heart, your mind,
and your soul. Because caring for yourself
makes you a more interesting,
interested person—and a better employee.

*C*onsultant and former J. Walter Thompson vice president Kevin Dolan thinks *workaholic* is a bad word, not a virtue. Dolan strongly believes in balance and equilibrium. He not only gives presentations on the subject to business people, he has devised a personal formula that consists of meditation, journal writing, nature walks, and more. He can show that this balanced lifestyle leads to an increase in productivity over the long haul.

John F. Raynolds III, the chairman and chief executive of Ward Howell International, has always known he needed "more than work in his life." So he balanced high-pressure jobs with the satisfaction of community volunteerism. He has concluded, "The saddest people are those who say they'll work hard and enjoy themselves when they retire. Those are the guys you find face down in the cornflakes."

The Eastern philosophies embrace a circle of life that balances the spiritual, emotional, physical, and mental. Nothing is separate from anything else: how we treat our family affects how well we work; how much exercise we get affects our creativity. The Western world tends to follow a more linear path. It's harder for us to see the relationship between disparate parts of our lives. Unless you're a fully developed human being you can't realize your full potential in the workplace.

The presidency of the United States has got to be the most demanding, time-intensive job in the country. But even the President takes time out to go running almost every day. If you were President, would you be apt to carve out R&R for yourself? How many hours a day do you think you'd be working?

No matter how busy they are, people always manage to find the time to spend a week in bed with the flu, or a month recovering from a heart attack. Have you considered finding the time to take a week while you're well? It could stave off major illness and a much longer involuntary vacation.

Snow monkeys work hard just to stay alive, climbing the mountains of northern Japan in search of food. But they take frequent breaks to rest and renew themselves. Evolution has taught them that all work and no play leads to extinction.

What you said about
BALANCED LIFESTYLE

The workaholic will burn out and ultimately cost us more money in the long run.

BROOK SMITH
First Vice President, RPR Corporate Finance

I believe employees need to be mindful of their personal priorities and reach their own goals. This makes for a better employee.

PATTIE CLAPP
Vice President, Govt. Relations, Greater Dallas Chamber of Commerce

---

With a family unit as a cornerstone and proper attention paid to those who really matter, a professional is far better able to both play hard and work hard—while all the time having fun.

BARRY NELSON
Principal, The Nelson Group

TOWARD VIRTUOSITY

What does balance mean to you? Does it mean putting in fewer hours at work? Or more hours into exercise? If you could define the "perfect" balance, what would it be?

———

Make a list of all the things you do on a weekly basis. Now, can you break the list down into family, work, physical, and spiritual headings? (Keep in mind that spiritual does not necessarily mean religious.)

———

Are you happy with your list? Are you spending your time the way you *want* to, as opposed to the way you *have* to? Is one section more exciting or dreary than another? Try to add or subtract activities, until each of the four sections represents its actual importance in your life.

———

Do you bring your work home with you, either in a briefcase or inside your own head? Try the blank notebook approach. Before you leave work each day (or night, as the case may be), write down any issues that may bother you after you get home. You may find that you can exorcise your work demons—leaving them bottled up in the notebook, until you open it up again the next morning.

CREATIVITY

Creativity doesn't mean being a *Picasso or da Vinci or even a Bill Gates, founder of Microsoft. Every day, everyone is a little creative, in lots of small ways. A receptionist who discovers a time-saving way to use the switchboard is using as much creativity as the head of research and development at a biotech company playing with* E. coli *bacteria.*

*O*ne boss defines a creative employee as someone able to think beyond the obvious. "If I tell her to go from A to B to C in order to reach D, she's liable to go from A to W and then back to her destination. That's very valuable, because people who manage businesses are often prisoners of their own reality. The creative person gives you another lens to look through, which energizes the dialogue, enriches the process, and makes the product better."

According to Harvard Business School's John Kao, creativity is "a major management agenda item for the 1990s."

Being creative doesn't necessarily mean reinventing the wheel. Small acts of creativity can be amazingly effective. And they tend to accumulate and gather momentum. When Mitzi Sales was in charge of the opening of a new building, she knew she'd have a problem with protesters—and that television crews would be there. She had to come up with a visual way to counter the pickets. Sales mobilized volunteers, put them all in white T-shirts, and gave them giant balloon bouquets. Everyone's eyes were drawn to the colorful balloons, and—especially because it was such a surprise—the protesters were lost in the festivities. On the TV coverage, all that anyone saw were white shirts and balloons.

Another example of a small creative stroke that made the drab world just a bit more fun: Russian immigrant Joseph Kaplan, who came to New York in 1901, saw plain old white shower curtains everywhere. So he started making shower curtains with colorful designs and fabrics. Obvious? Sure. Most creative ideas are obvious *after* someone's pointed them out.

Bruce Blackburn has his own graphic design firm, which often does annual reports. When the CEO of a computer company said, "I don't want any pictures in my report, I want only words," Blackburn thought, "What a loser!" But finally he decided to turn himself over to his client's direction. Making pictures out of words, Blackburn designed a series of annual reports that had no actual photographs. He used charts as illustrations, devoted full pages to six or seven quotations or facts, ranged against a grid, all the same typeface and weight. It was organized looking, yet random. Blackburn won awards for his "great insight."

———

"I used to think that anyone doing anything weird *was* weird. I suddenly realized that anyone doing anything weird wasn't weird at all and it was the people saying they were weird that was weird." Paul McCartney

———

What does algebra have to do with creativity? Not as much as geometry, according to the president and founder of a market research firm. Skye Hallberg prefers employees who are better at geometry than algebra. Why? "I need people who are creative," Hallberg said. "Creativity has to come from the paradigm from which you look at business. Geometry has more to do with spatial perception. I don't look for geometry geniuses, but art directors and other creative people tend to be good at geometry."

———

Creative employees tend to carve out their own roles in business, sometimes even at a tender age. Robb Gaynor is a twenty-seven-year-old manager at Charles Schwab, and creativity got him there. "We called him Boy Wonder," says the man who hired him. "He'd race off on his own and come back with ideas outside his job area." As Gaynor's most recent boss describes him, "If you're looking for someone to deliver a report every week, you don't want Robb. But for creative ideas and making things happen, he's terrific."

Studies have shown that people are at their most creative at age five. Maybe that's why some well-known painters including Gauguin and Paul Klee used children's drawings as inspiration for works of art that now hang in museums.

"The creative person wants to be a know-it-all. He wants to know about all kinds of things: ancient history, nineteenth-century mathematics, current manufacturing techniques, flower arranging, and hog futures. Because he never knows when these ideas might come together to form a new idea. It may happen six minutes later or six months down the road. But he has faith that it will happen." Carl Ally, founder, Ally & Gargano Advertising Agency

What you said about
CREATIVITY

Seventeen percent of the executives we surveyed ranked being creative as one of the five top business virtues. They were from diverse geographic areas and both large and small companies.

Of those who chose creativity as the number one virtue, the largest percentage came from the southwest, followed by the west coast and the midwest.

We are a small biotech company with limited financial resources. If we are to compete successfully against the pharmaceutical giants we must rely on our ability to be more creative and to make decisions more rapidly — and to provide an environment where this is likely.

DAVID DEWEESE
President and CEO, MG Pharmaceuticals, Inc.

Creativity is the key to our specialty company's success… Very few of our problems have simple straightforward solutions. They require creative solutions which avoid "no" answers to our customers.

RICHARD KENNEY
President and CEO, Crown Textile Co.

Being creative is the fuel of the future. Change occurs moment by moment, and being creative is the only way to ensure success in the long term.

BRUCE MANDELBILT
Treasurer, L.I.I.

Creativity—With it most challenges can be met. Without it, problems are seldom converted into opportunities.

DAVID FAGIN
Chairman and CEO, Golden Star Resources, Ltd.

TOWARD VIRTUOSITY

Creativity is a muscle. It gets better with exercise. If you don't stretch, it will atrophy. Start by practicing in easy areas, like cooking without a recipe, or arranging photographs on a wall, or playing with the fonts on your Mac. Then work your way up.

Sherlock Holmes used to tell Watson that the best way to find the solution was to eliminate every answer that must be wrong—the only remaining candidate must be the right answer. The same approach can work for you. Write down every possible idea, no matter how ridiculous. Then eliminate the impossible and pursue the rest.

List the most obvious solution to the biggest obstacles in your current project. Now think of two other approaches you've never considered before. If you find this difficult, pretend you're someone else who is completely unlike you. How would Robin Williams solve the problem? Isaac Asimov? Superman? Be as outrageous and unrealistic as you can.

Who is the most creative person you know personally? How does he/she spend time? What habits does he/she have?

Find a placc reserved exclusively for creative thought—perhaps a room, a park bench, a special chair in the library—which you use only when trying to solve problems. You'll set up a conditioned response, where your creative juices start flowing as you walk in.

Learn to brainstorm. Gather some colleagues and force yourself to identify *dozens* of wacky ideas—but restrain yourself from negative feedback: "That'll never work" is not allowed.

Sometimes we fall into sensory ruts: we think only verbally or only visually. If you tend to be linear in your thinking, experiment with drawing Venn diagrams (those intersecting circles you learned in math class). If you doodle a lot, try word games. Make up as many new words out of the letters in your name as you can, for instance.

CURIOSITY

World-class competitor Motorola *requires every employee to take more than forty hours of classes a year, ranging from statistics to pottery—on company time.*

Never hurts to ask. Hallberg Schireson, a marketing firm, had an account with a company that was known for its stain, but wanted to sell more of its paint. The first thing Hallberg asked was why their paint was $17 a gallon when other, similar paints were only $14 a gallon. Nobody at the paint company seemed to know. The research and development people said, "We use more expensive ingredients." Hallberg asked, "Why?" R&D said, "There's some ingredient in there that's better, but we're not sure what it does." Hallberg said, "Can you tell us anything more about this ingredient?" R&D said, "No, but we know it exceeds some sort of federal standards." Finally, the marketers took it upon themselves to look up these federal standards in a very thick manual on the subject. They found that 80 percent of paint jobs are over previously painted surfaces. Even better, they discovered that the expensive ingredient made paint stick better to previously painted surfaces. So, where the research and development department had dropped the ball, Hallberg found a perfect reason why Olympic paint was more expensive and why it was worth every extra penny. End result of all this curiosity? Sales soared.

"You've got to *grab* that garbanzo bean!" So said food writer M.F.K. Fisher, who exhorted young people to learn everything they could from every experience. "Even if it's just a garbanzo bean," she would say, "you never know when it will come in handy."

Sumner Redstone could have stopped being curious years ago. He already owned a highly successful theater chain. He had everything a person could possibly want. But, at age 63, he began buying stock in a fledgling cable company. "I knew nothing about cable, nothing about music networks or programming, either. But I went around asking everyone questions until I got the answers." The result? Today Redstone is the titan of the cable industry, owner of Viacom, a multibillion-dollar company.

Twelve years ago, Delta Wire Company had ten employees. Today, it has 125 employees, wins major industry awards, and is in the midst of a $2.5 million expansion—after a $2 million expansion last year. The secret to the company's success? Since 1985 president George Walker has paid workers at their regular hourly rate—double the local average—to attend classes in everything from basic skills to statistics, in order to compete in a global economy.

Microsoft founder Bill Gates is probably the wealthiest man in America today. So what kind of employee does he look for to run his divisions? "We're not looking for any specific knowledge," Gates said, "because things change so fast, and it's easy to learn stuff. You've got to have an excitement about software, a certain intelligence and a willingness to work with a group of people to define where software should go. If somebody's never played around much with a personal computer, they're probably not a very good candidate, because they're not likely to be very curious. It's not like the specific knowledge counts, but where have you been?—aren't you intrigued, don't you think it's fascinating what they can do, what they can't do, where they will go, what does it mean?"

John F. Raynolds III, chairman of Ward Howell International, wasn't always the head of a prestigious recruiting firm. Years ago, he wangled a job in investment banking, athough he knew almost nothing about financial analysis. He quickly realized he was in over his head. But instead of panicking or quitting or cheating, he simply "attached myself to some of the hotshots at the company and learned." In fact, he learned so well that within a few years he became an executive vice president of the parent company.

—————

The national director of financial planning at Price Waterhouse believes that the key to success in business is learning from your mistakes. Carol Caruthers said, "People don't remember your mistakes; they remember what you made from them."

What you said about
CURIOSITY

A third of survey respondents ranked always learning and curious as a top virtue.

Among CEOs, 19 percent checked curious and always learning; 30 percent of company presidents thought it was important.

—————

The ability to learn is critical. We can hire employees with ability but current lack of knowledge and then train them. We cannot utilize employees who do not respond to training through lack of their internal capacity and motivation to learn.

BERYL FARRIS
Beryl Farris and Peter Hill Law Office

TOWARD VIRTUOSITY

How often do you ask yourself, "Why do they do it that way?"

How many magazines do you read a month? How many of those are outside your usual interests? Try buying a magazine every few weeks that's totally unrelated to your job or hobbies. A campaign manager who wanted to start a cable company impressed investors with his knowledge of the new industry—attained by reading dozens of trade magazines on cable.

Nothing sparks curiosity better than browsing. Give yourself a treat: spend an afternoon at your local library or a good bookstore, with no particular goal in mind. Let your mind wander wherever it seems to want to go. Find yourself in the ancient history section? Check out a book. Go ahead. Now bring it home and read it! Or at least read part of it.

Act like a four-year-old. Question everything. Try asking someone "Why?" five or six times in a row and watch how the complicated suddenly becomes simple.

Look around your workplace. Who knows more than you do? Pick their brains, take them to lunch, ask them to tutor you, flatter them about their expertise. You'll learn a lot.

Do you know what you don't know? Make a list, then start crossing things off as you learn them.

DRIVE

Drive doesn't mean to be a *workaholic. Nor does it mean to be unethical. The executives we spoke with see drive as a combination of goal-setting, focus, engagement, and competitiveness. They all agreed that crossing the line from these positive attributes to cheating your family, your colleagues, or yourself leads to failure.*

*D*onna Karan, the celebrated fashion designer and founder of DKNY, started out in the business as Anne Klein's assistant. While pregnant with her first child, she made it clear to Klein that she was committed to the business as much as her own and her baby's health would permit. Anne Klein died when Karan's baby was two days old. The company's corporate head asked Karan to take over as chief designer.

———

Does drive conflict with a balanced lifestyle? Not necessarily. On the golf course, Jack Nicklaus is as driven as they come. But he's managed to build a multimillion-dollar business at the same time, raise a great family, and find his inner satisfaction.

———

Often drive is the only difference between champions and losers. As star golfer Nancy Lopez once said, "Competitors take bad breaks and use them to drive themselves just that much harder. Quitters take bad breaks and use them as reasons to give up."

———

Ella Williams started her own defense contracting firm in 1981 with a loan from the Small Business Administration, maxed out her credit cards and took a second mortgage on her house. For the first three years, she failed to drum up any business. Where a lesser woman might have quit, she stuck with it, even sweetening the pot by sending home-baked goods to prospects. Finally, she landed an $8 million contract with the Naval Air Warfare Center. Since then, she has been named the 1993 AT&T Entrepreneur of the Year; the SBA's Small Business Prime Contractor of the Year in 1989 and 1990; and the Outstanding Small Business Subcontractor of the Year in 1986. "I don't want women to think I'm some kind of superwoman," Williams cautioned. "I'm real, and anyone can do what I've done if they have the determination and drive."

———

Alphonse Fletcher, the twenty-eight-year-old CEO and founder of Fletcher Asset Management, has always followed his grandmother's preacher's advice: "Bite off more than you can chew. Then chew it."

What you said about
DRIVE

Drive encompasses so many important attributes. High drive, energy, ethics, and intelligence are a great combination.

DARLENE ORLOV
President, Orlov Resources

TOWARD VIRTUOSITY

No one just wakes up one morning and becomes driven. You need to take it a little at a time. Here's an effective technique. Circle a day on your calendar a few days away. Decide that for one day—eight full hours at work—you'll be driven. Start preparing. Clean your desk. Make a list of what you'd like to accomplish. Schedule every minute of the day ruthlessly. Go to bed early the night before, wear your best clothes, get to work early.

After you've amazed yourself (and your boss) with what you can accomplish in just one day, you'll understand what it is to be driven.

On a scale of one to ten, rank yourself on focus, goal-setting, and competitiveness. If you're not committed to these three elements, you're not operating at full speed.

––––––––

Who's your role model when it comes to drive? Is there someone in your company or your family who combines intensity and focus with the ability to hang on for the long haul? How do they do it?

––––––––

It's hard to be driven if you can't keep score. Figure out what you're trying to accomplish—number of sales calls made, good reviews garnered, or units produced. It'll make it easier to top yourself next time.

EFFICIENCY

I f you don't have time to do it right,
when will you find time to do it over?

*E*fficiency doesn't mean hard work. It means smart work. An efficient manager can run a multibillion-dollar company in the same time it takes Joe to make a day's worth of sandwiches at the corner deli.

One of IBM chairman and chief exec Louis V. Gerstner's main goals is to reorganize the behemoth company to make it run more efficiently. Changes are noticeable at all levels. Managers who were accustomed for years to presenting heavy blue binder reports complete with overhead projector slides at meetings were required to submit reports no longer than five pages on such broad topics as what they did and who their markets were. And, in response to e-mail complaints from a software programmer on all the red tape he encountered just to get a software program that was developed by another department, Gerstner issued an edict ordering all IBM departments to share their software enthusiastically and free of charge. Supporters and critics alike are impressed by Gerstner's ability to act quickly and streamline operations.

Henry Ford did not like to waste time. One way he avoided doing so was always to consult with his colleagues in their own offices rather than in his. He realized it was much easier for him to "leave the other fellow's office than I can get him to leave mine."

Organizational consultant Harrison Owen developed the concept of "open-space" meetings as a way for companies to expose problems and create more efficient operating systems. Employees are invited to write down comments, opinions, or questions about anything that is on their minds. These are tacked to the wall as sign-up sheets and turned into topics for discussion groups. Recommendations are made and committees formed to follow them through. The Rockport Company's distribution center saw immediate results from Harrison's organizational meetings. Training specialists were hired, e-mail installed, an employee directory created, and a company newsletter distributed. Workers are happier and efficiency was enhanced.

"I would I could stand on a busy corner, hat in hand, and beg people to throw me all their wasted hours." Bernard Berenson, 1865–1959, art critic and historian

---

Andrew Tobias, best-selling investment book author, uses call waiting to great advantage. He'll interrupt a conversation to take a message from the second caller, but will always return to the original caller—no matter how important the new call is. It keeps things straight, and he doesn't have to worry about slighting anyone.

Successful entrepreneur Sam Attenberg sets aside several hours a day in which he won't take phone calls. That way, Attenberg said, "I work according to my own schedule, not my callers' convenience."

What you said about
EFFICIENCY

~◆~

Mother used to tell me "if I didn't use my head I'd use my feet." An organized person not only is able to work effectively but respects the time of others—both superiors and subordinates. Most people appreciate such consideration.

TOM QUALEY JR.
CEO and Owner, Jefferson Davis Nursing Home

Efficient—important to be able to prioritize and get the most important tasks done in the least amount of time.

JOHN RINGE
Partner, Peat Marwick

Because of the amount of paperwork in the various aspects of the company (grounds, pro shop, payroll, etc.), organizing is a key talent. Anything can be accomplished when one is organized.

TRINA HESS
Manager, Hi-Level Golf Course

TOWARD VIRTUOSITY

~◆~

Time is your most valuable asset. How are you using it? Do you keep an organizer or a to-do list? Don't fool yourself into thinking you can run an organized life without writing anything down.

———————

If you have a secretary, enlist his/her help. Have him/her enforce your schedule and be sure that you're using your time wisely.

———————

Try to touch each piece of paper only once as it crosses your desk. Decide right away how to dispose of it, either through acting, delegating, filing, or tossing.

———————

Work within your own rhythms for maximum efficiency. When you know you're at your peak, tackle the most challenging parts of your job. If you don't wake up for the first hour after you arrive at the office, plan mindless tasks for that period. If you get too drowsy right after lunch, do the most physical part of your job then.

———————

Push the envelope with your computer. Get e-mail. Use it. Computerize your mailing lists, address books, calendars, and any other repetitive tasks that computers are more efficient at. But be sure you don't computerize tasks that are better done by hand.

———————

Every morning, make a list of what you want to accomplish that day. Then rank each item in order of importance.

ETHICS

Is *business ethics* an oxymoron?
Defining ethics can be as difficult as
practicing ethics. The executives we spoke to
mentioned fairness, honesty, conscience,
and the golden rule.

Well-known pollster Burns Roper is famous for his ethical standards, especially when it comes to the interpretation of polls by clients. Sometimes clients abuse good research by taking it out of context, releasing some portions and not others, or by using it to make misleading advertising claims. "We've blown the whistle on some clients," Roper said. "It's a painful thing to do, but it has to be done." The upside for Roper? Any poll bearing his name has credibility.

"It's not just whether it's legal or illegal; it's whether it's right or wrong." That's how Ralph Giannola, vice president of marketing, Marriott Corporation, defines ethical. Tom Peters is more specific: "High ethical standards—business or otherwise—are, above all, about treating people decently. To me that means respect for a person's opinions, privacy, background, dignity, and natural desire to grow."

In a recent study, more than 80 percent of executives said they believed managers choose profits over what's right, when forced to decide between the two.

The Hippocratic Oath, at two thousand years old, is probably one of the oldest written codes of ethics for any profession. Named after Hippocrates, rather than created by him, the oath probably owes its long existence to the fact that it provides a flexible framework for medical ethics instead of a rigid set of rules.

According to Malcolm Forbes Jr., Dial Corporation CEO John Teets "epitomizes the kind of person corporate America needs more of today." Not only did Teets help Dial's bottom line soar, he has done so in an admirable way. Forbes wrote of him, "He is the opposite of the cold, hard-hearted CEO ensconced in an isolated executive suite. Personal tragedies and early obstacles have made him deeply spiritual. His Horatio Alger–like rise from mean circumstances has deepened his humanity rather than snuffed it out. He is generous. He takes a keen personal interest in the people who work for him. He demonstrates that commerce and religion are not incompatible and, in fact, that religion can help an executive be more sensitive to the needs of others, which is the essence of business—fulfilling the needs and desires of customers in an ethical manner."

The best and brightest, of course, realize that putting ethical behavior first often results in better business. Nowhere is this more clearly demonstrated than in the advertising world. In the earliest days of Victorian advertising there were some extraordinary examples of snake oil–type promotion. But those who built the great brands like Kellogg's or Campbell's were careful not to overpromise, not to deceive, not to mislead, even accidentally. They wanted to be around for a long time. And they still are here.

Kevin Dolan was with J. Walter Thompson advertising for almost twenty-five years. One of his favorite stories is about Norman Strauss, chairman of the agency in the early 1960s. RCA gave Strauss a new reel-to-reel tape recorder to advertise. Strauss marched into RCA's CEO and announced that the machine chewed up tape and turned it into spaghetti. Strauss said, "The product doesn't work. We can't advertise it." The RCA CEO replied, "If that's your point of view, we'll give some other agency the entire RCA account." Strauss turned to walk out the door. "Wait a minute," shouted the RCA chief. "If you feel so strongly you're willing to sacrifice the whole account, it must be a bad product. We'll fix it." So J. Walter Thompson kept the account. Dolan, who was standing outside the door holding Strauss's bag, said it made an enormous impression on him because it stood for the integrity of the company.

Later, when Dolan had become deputy head of J. Walter Thompson's international accounts, Frederick's of Hollywood, the purveyor of sexy lingerie, wanted to give him its international account. "Turned out they needed our good name," said Dolan. "I told them that's exactly the reason we wouldn't handle it—if we gave Frederick's our name it would no longer stand for a certain ethical standard."

"Company CEOs spend 90 percent of their lives making their companies look good for investors, not being good," wrote Peter Senge. "Managers spend their lives making their little departments look good, not working for the good of the company."

What you said about
ETHICS

This virtue outranked every other one on our survey list by far. Fifty percent of respondents said not only was being ethical the most important virtue, but that without it, none of the others mattered. Now, we don't know whether this means business types really are ethical; really want to be ethical; or merely think they are supposed to be ethical. But the fact that so many people would like to think of themselves as ethical is significant.

Ethical behavior is the cornerstone of free enterprise. If employees are not ethical, no amount of supervision or training can change them. And the consequences of unethical actions are lost customer trust/confidence, and lost sales!

CAROLYN YOCH
Vice President, Kraft USA

Ethical to me means having a sense of what's just and fair. So it includes most of the other virtues: responsibility; the capacity to put things in a right order; accountability; a sense of what needs to be done and what it will take to do it; empathy (compassion); courage; imagination; and balanced priorities.

GARY HAUCK
Secretary of the University, Emory University

A person who embodies a sound value system will, to the highest degree possible, exhibit loyalty, organization, esprit de corps and a reasonable degree of intelligence, to be a "total person."

BILL KRAFT
CEO, Healthcare System

Regardless of the length and breadth of the other virtues, achievements and accomplishments will be shallow and short term without employers and co-workers who possess the virtue of ethics.

TERRY SIDLOW
Vice President, College of American Pathologists

TOWARD VIRTUOSITY

Secrecy is the ally of the unethical businessperson. The more public you are about your actions, the more likely you are to act ethically.

Every field has ethical leaders—those who are like a litmus test for others to measure their actions against. Who are your ethical leaders? Pick one and try to emulate his or her behavior.

There's one foolproof way to know what the most ethical choice in any situation is: what would you want your kids to know you'd done?

List ten incidents in your work life when you had to make an ethics-based decision. Did you do the right thing? Were your actions fair or unfair? Legal or illegal? What did you do? Why? If you had it to do over again, would you still make the same choice? If you made an unethical choice, how was it affected your career?

Find a sounding board. It's often difficult to make the right decision when faced with business pressures and deadlines. Is there someone you can call and ask for advice? Sometimes, you'll discover that verbalizing the dilemma is all you need to make the right decision on your own.

FEARLESSNESS

In business you cannot discover
new heights unless you have the
courage to leave the ground.

*T*he story of Omar Aziz and his New Orleans Famous Omar Pies is one of true fearlessness. Omar plunged into pies and grew too fast. Unfortunately, the bottom dropped out. Not willing to quit without a fight, Aziz went back to college and studied hard to find the right way to build and market his business. In 1989, he resurrected it, and it has been growing ever since.

The chairman and CEO of IBM, Louis V. Gerstner, was quoted on the subject of risk-taking: "There are no recipes...There are no certainties...You've got to go on instinct."

Tom Peters is passionate about fearlessness. He believes that people who try but make mistakes should be promoted, while those that never even attempt to fail should be fired. After all, the fearless people are learning. They're also the employees who are taking the company to new levels of excellence.

When Clorox asked a market research firm to sell its new wintergreen cat litter, it was a product ahead of its time. It also cost twice as much as other litters. The executive in charge of the account recalled, "We had to figure out a way to reposition the product, and I was really excited when I came up with the idea of kitten litter, instead of cat litter. Then I held a focus group. One of the pet owners said there was no difference between cats and kittens when it came to litter. My wonderful idea was shot down. So we established the Try Something Award, for the best bad idea. In order to have good ideas you have to be willing to fail."

"Most people who come into Andersen spend the next ten years working...in whatever divison they were originally assigned to," according to Liz Landon. At age twenty–nine, Landon already has worked in three different areas as a consultant at Andersen Consulting, which has almost thirty thousand employees. So how does her boss and managing partner characterize her rapid rise and unusual career path? "She is almost fearless to try anything."

"No passion so effectually robs the mind of all its power of acting and reasoning as fear." Edmund Burke, 1729-1797

A few years ago, Berkeley Repertory Theater was in the process of building a new theater. Arts patron Mark Taper, then in his eighties, preferred to give funding to organizations that would name buildings after him. When Taper heard Berkeley Rep was looking for large donors, he called the theater's business manager to announce he would give them $100,000 if they would name the main stage after Mark Taper. Now at this time the largest gift the theater had ever received was $10,000. But the business manager took a deep breath, considered the risks, and then said, "No, we couldn't possibly do that for less than $250,000." She got her money.

What you said about
FEARLESSNESS

Because we are a start-up company deploying a new technology, we must all be fearless in order to do our jobs day-to-day.

KIM NORRIS
Director of Marketing, OneComm

Fearless: It is important that a person can stand up for his thoughts, plans, ideas, etc., and make a case for them no matter the opposition or consequences.

MELVIN SILVER
President, Charmel Systems

Fearless, more so than visionary. Many have the ability to look at events and trends and describe a future state. However, few are willing to take the risks of acting on that vision unless the current state is bad. To reform or change tactics that a change are working, based on your vision of the future, requires courage.

ANDREW POWELL
Manager, Human Resources, BF Goodrich

TOWARD VIRTUOSITY

If you focus on the negative outcomes of every action, you're certain to become paralyzed by fear. If you want to take a risk, think in terms of worst-case scenarios. If you do X, what's the absolute worst thing that could happen? Once you've written down your worst outcome, it's easier to focus on the benefits of your actions.

Nothing is as powerful as the condition of nothing to lose. If you've got no downside, why not give it a try?

Make a list of three ways you could be more fearless at work. What's holding you back? Write down all the obstacles or bad consequences of your actions. Now, write down the costs of being fearful.

One way to encourage yourself to take risks is to announce your actions as a fait accompli. Tell a co-worker, "Tomorrow, I'm going to bring this new proposal to Mr. Fendrick!" And you've added peer pressure to your resolve. The best way to *dis*courage yourself from taking risks is to look for permission, by asking, "Should I show this to Mr. Fendrick?" If your colleagues were fearless, they'd already be promoted!

Try visualization. Imagine yourself as a samurai warrior, an astronaut, or Nancy Drew. One woman we know had an undershirt printed for her husband's first day at a fiercely competitive new job. It said, "Killer Fish."

FOCUS

Mountain climbers, undercover
espionage agents, and race car drivers don't
daydream very often. Something about
risking death f̶o̶r̶c̶e̶s̶ ̶t̶h̶e̶s̶e̶ ̶d̶a̶r̶e̶d̶e̶v̶i̶l̶s̶ on
the essentials of the present.

B	*e here now.* When you focus, then your own skills, attributes, and virtues all come into play. When you are fully engaged in the present, the best you can do occurs spontaneously, which is all anyone needs to succeed.

"I relate being engaged with being passionate about work." That's how public relations firm owner Katherine McDonough defined this virtue. She explained, "We work with media all over the world, with many clients outside the U.S. Once a French client was going to be in a *New York Times* story the next day. My employees went down to the *Times* at 9:30 that night and faxed the story to Paris so the client would have it that same morning. Everyone wants to do well and get a good performance review. But understanding what the client needed and taking the initiative, even though it was inconvenient, goes beyond. When you're engaged, you connect with your work beyond keeping score, or getting the job done. You connect on an extremely personal level which produces an enthusiasm and creativity that makes the work extremely satisfying."

No one has made more impact or more money by being engaged than Bill Gates of Microsoft. In meetings, Gates is constantly in motion. As he thinks, his body rocks back and forth, back and forth, an involuntary coupling of his mind and body. It's natural for him—he's not wearing a mask. Gates has absorbed his business into his bloodstream. Because his business decisions are an extension of his personal decisions, he has no trouble acting swiftly and consistently.

"Life cannot wait until the sciences have explained the universe scientifically. We cannot put off living until we are ready. The most salient characteristic of life is its coerciveness: it is always urgent, here and now without any possible postponement. Life is fired at us point blank." José Ortega y Gasset, writer

---

The father of quality organizations, W. Edwards Deming, advocated discontinuing all merit systems and never graded his own students. Why? Because Deming felt that "You cannot enjoy doing a job only to beat someone else; if you don't enjoy doing the job, you cannot contribute to a quality organization."

Viacom chairman Sumner Redstone said, "Great successes are built on taking the negatives in your life, the challenges and frustrations, and turning them around. Taking a negative and turning it into a positive. Overcoming hazard. Overcoming danger. Overcoming catastrophe."

Zig Ziglar describes the typical executive as one who spends his days at work thinking about being with his family, and his time at home thinking about work: "No wonder he doesn't get anything done...he's always traveling!"

Every year, Domino's has a company-wide contest for the fastest pizza maker. Employees train year round to develop just the right technique to take a pizza from dough to the table in the least amount of time. The contest helps the pizza wizards stay focused.

In the novel *Zorba the Greek*, the author tells this story: "Zorba came upon an old man planting an apricot seedling and asked why he, an old man, was planting a new tree. 'I live as though I would never die,' was his reply. 'And me, I live as though I might die tomorrow,' said Zorba. 'Which one of us is right?' "

What you said about
FOCUS

Employees who are focused can produce credible results, deepen their understanding of interrelationships, become compassionate, and finally realize that success is a journey and not a destination.

JOSEPH GORMAN
Chairman, Olympic Industries Inc.

If you are not focused you will not meet or exceed the duties and responsibilities of your position.

FREDERICK ALLEY
President and CEO, The Brooklyn Hospital Center

Focus is critical in my company because competition is keen and the industry is highly rewarded—therefore extraneous distractions must not prevail.

DOUGLAS GRAHAM
Senior Vice President and Corporate Personnel Director,
Regions Financial Corp.

Focused—because this virtue above all others helps the institution to achieve results.

JERRY COTTON
Associate Director, Mississippi Baptist Medical

TOWARD VIRTUOSITY

What do you do when your mind starts to wander? Are you aware of it?

Human beings find it very difficult to keep their thoughts from being like monkeys jumping all over the place. Assess how well you are able to stay focused on the present. One second? Ten seconds? A minute? Once you are aware of how much of the time you're not in the present, you can practice gently reminding yourself to come back to the present when you're way out in the future or stuck in the past.

It's very hard to feel engaged if you aren't being stimulated enough. Yet when things are too challenging, you can feel frustrated or overwhelmed. The key is the right balance between effort and result in each of your tasks. A job needs to require concentration or you'll soon be bored. But even a hamburger flipper at McDonald's can make his job more rewarding. How can you make your job more interesting?

The least engaging activity ever designed is television. Not only are you totally passive when you spend time gazing at the tube, but it often takes hours to clear your mind of TV's numbing images. It's like brain pollution. For one week, turn off the television and watch what happens to your mind.

GOALS

No one was less surprised to be *appointed vice president of Ford Motor Company at the age of thirty-six than Lee Iacocca. After all, while still in college at Lehigh University he had decided to become a Ford vice president—by age thirty-five.*

*E*ffective goal setting requires four elements: a specific, measurable goal; a date for completion; a list of the benefits that will accrue to you for reaching the goal and, finally, a realistic assessment of what you'll need to learn in order to reach your goal.

"To tend, unfailingly, unflinchingly, towards a goal, is the secret of success." Anna Pavlova, 1881–1931, Russian ballerina

---

When Gordon Crane founded Apple and Eve juice company, his goal was to maintain the highest quality product, no matter how large the company grew. "We stick to our knitting," said Crane. "It's the basics. We're fanatical about quality, and we've kept our eyes glued to the marketplace." Toward that goal, Crane still samples every new batch of juice before it's bottled, and reads about one hundred consumer letters every week.

"The carpenter's rule is 'measure twice, cut once.' You have to make sure that the blueprint, the first creation, is really what you want, that you've thought everything through. Then you put it into brick and mortar. Each day you go to the construction shed and pull out the blueprint to get marching orders for the day. You begin with the end in mind." Stephen Covey, best-selling author

---

Abraham Lincoln ran for city council, state legislator, governor, and Congress. He lost every election. Fortunately for us, he didn't decide to "just give politics a shot and see what happens." He persisted and ultimately succeeded, because he had a clear goal.

"A winner is someone who recognizes his God-given talents, works his tail off to develop into skills, and uses these skills to accomplish goals." Larry Bird, basketball player

_____

When Columbus set sail, you can bet that he didn't tell his crew, "Let's just sail around for a while and see if we find anything interesting." While this sounds ridiculous, it's exactly what many businesses and employees do every day.

_____

Japan has shown the effectiveness of an entire nation setting goals. Since 1960, the government has set decade-long goals, targeting specific industries for dominance. Since beginning its national goals program, Japan has risen from a third-rate power to the country with the largest per capita trade surplus in the history of the world.

_____

A less positive example of the effects of national goal setting: Why was the United States so much more effective at motivating itself to fight World War II than the Vietnam War? One reason is that our goals in Vietnam were never clearly stated, and our progress, therefore, was difficult to measure. And as William G. Dyer, of Brigham Young University, once explained, "Goals should be specific, realistic, and measurable."

_____

ABCDEFG...ABCDEFGHIJ...Imagine how much harder it would be for a toddler to master the alphabet if, after every mistake, he started over from the beginning. Goals provide a way to deal with minor setbacks by keeping our eyes on the ultimate destination.

_____

"Too often people mistake being busy for achieving goals."
Philip D. Harvey, founder, Population Services International,
and James D. Snyder, president, Snyder Associates, Inc.

What you said about
GOALS

*The health insurance industry is going through major
changes and to survive people will need to be able to set and
achieve goals.*

TERENCE ZASTROW
Director, The Mutual Group

*Goals help to crystallize your thinking. Develop plans and
deadlines; develop sincere desire to achieve; develop confidence and determination.*

FLOYD KEITH
Head Football Coach, University of Rhode Island

*In these confusing times it is essential that employees are
focused upon the principal goals of the enterprise.*

JERRY SENNE
Vice President, VHA Inc.

*Holding executives responsible for achieving their yearly
goals is critical to a company's success.*

DAN O'NEIL
Executive Vice President, Wayne Lambert & Co.

TOWARD VIRTUOSITY

Have you written down your goals? If not, then you haven't completed the most important motivational task. Give yourself twenty-four hours, then write a document that outlines goals for three time frames: daily, weekly, or monthly; annual; and five years. Your unconscious mind is an incredibly powerful tool. Presenting it with a set of written goals will allow it to discover new and effective ways to accomplish the things you *really* want.

Making New Year's resolutions is one approach to goals. A variation on this theme is to turn it into a more fun, positive ritual. One couple we know never goes out on New Year's Eve. Instead, they get together with champagne, finger food, and their calendars, checkbooks, and diaries for the past year. They make a list of highlights, divided into individual, couple, family, and professional. Then they decide on a few areas they want to work on the upcoming year, from writing a book to running a marathon. Each New Year's they check the previous year's list.

Do your goals conflict? You can't bill more hours than anyone else in your law firm *and* spend more time with your family.

Does your company have written goals? Can your employees or managers recite them if you ask?

Grace Under
PRESSURE

How does an NFL referee cope with *the pressure of 80,000 screaming fans? By keeping his perspective. He knows that fans won't kill or injure him just for making a bad call. Every day, managers, executives and referees face more pressure than you could imagine, yet they don't crack.*

*S*ome companies are trying to reduce employee stress on a day-to-day basis—before it gets out of control. Chiat Day in Los Angeles, following the Japanese model, set up a club room, where workers can play pool or spar with punching bags decorated with the faces of the agency's top executives. Other companies run indoor golf tournaments or allow their employees to paint their work spaces in wild colors.

The chief executive of Norand Corporation, which makes hand-held computers, got his job by being graceful under pressure. In 1982 he was recruited by Donaldson, Lufkin and Jenrette to resuscitate a manufacturing company in northern California. Although the company failed, Robert Hammer impressed DLJ folks a lot. "In adversity you learn lots of things about people," said a DLJ spokesman. "No matter how difficult things got, Hammer never lied. He was scrappy, he worked through problems without flailing around. Always cool. We saw how he worked when things were tough. We wanted to put him into a situation where things could be good." And so they went out and bought Norand just for him.

"Never promise more than you can perform." Publilius Syrus, 42 B.C., Roman writer

Personnel executive Kevin Dolan defined the opposite of grace under pressure: "I've had bosses who were cordial and affable—until stress hit. Then they would become obnoxious and abrasive. When men are threatened with failure, they can revert to almost animalistic behavior."

Chuck Ballard, general manager for a New York sales region, is a seasoned executive. Last year his division was struggling to meet its sales quota. The chairman put tremendous pressure on Ballard's marketing team to sell the company's services. So the team really killed themselves to make the sales, which would result in hefty year-end bonuses for all. But, despite Ballard's efforts, the chairman really waxed into him, deeply wounding Ballard's pride. Turned out the company Christmas party was held the same day. Ballard was able to lift himself above his boss's temper tantrum and give a very moving speech on what a great team he had. Of course one knowledgeable guest said it was that double martini she had given him. But most of his co-workers knew he is a perfect example of grace under pressure.

When Jeffrey C. Barbakow took over as chairman of National Medical Enterprises in 1993, the company was the subject of a federal criminal investigation as well as civil charges. After six hundred FBI agents raided twenty company facilities for documents, the stock fell another 30 percent in one day. Barbakow, however, realized that the furor wasn't about him, it was about his company. By separating the two, he was able to depersonalize the pressure and remain calm. He got on the phone with bankers and analysts to discuss his plan to salvage the company. The stock rebounded, and settlements and deals followed.

What you said about
GRACE UNDER PRESSURE

Investment banking is an intense business. There are many intelligent and honest people, but those who are successful in our business are those that perform at their best when under the most pressure.

MITCHELL SPECTOR
Associate Director, Bear, Stearns & Co.

Grace under pressure reflects self-confidence and flexibility while exuding an aura of effortless execution. Such determination comes easy when you know what you are doing—others recognize this and respect your knowledge, skills and abilities.

DAVID SHULMAN
Associate, Perot Systems Corporation

At this time in our company as we recover from some serious scandals, the ability to admit mistakes, make important recompensation gestures, and still perform the recovery well, on your feet, ready to carry on with head held high—that is a virtue!

JAMES RUSSELL
Vice President, Metropolitan Life Insurance Company

TOWARD VIRTUOSITY

When stressful circumstances mount, try to think about what will be important in five years or even five weeks—not just in the next five minutes.

Sports often have moments of high intensity, yet players virtually always survive. Find a game like tennis, squash, or fencing that will allow you to train your mind to transcend intermittent periods of high stress.

Parents often use "time-outs" for their misbehaving kids. The technique works equally well for grownups. The next time you're about to lose your temper, take a time-out for yourself. Adjourn the meeting for a few minutes, or find a reason to return the phone call. Leave the room, walk around the block, put on that Sony Walkman.

Emulate the most dignified, courteous people you can think of. Imagine how Jacqueline Kennedy Onassis, Lena Horne, or Fred Astaire would behave in your situation.

Don't let your reaction to pressure get personal. Focus on behavior and situations, not people. Instead telling an employee, "How could you be so spacy that you missed such an important deadline?" try "I'm very disappointed that we missed the deadline. How can I help avoid this situation next time?"

HARD WORK

Tom Pavela often arrives at Apple *Computer long before anyone else, so he can get serious work done in the quiet morning hours. He points out that staying late implies that you couldn't finish all your work during the day, while coming in early means that you just want to get a jump on things.*

A young man began his career as a clerk in a department store. Immediately upon finishing lunch with a co-worker one day, he got up to go back to work. The co-worker told him to take his time. The young man ignored this advice. Within two months he was manager of the whole store. His name? J.C. Penney. Eventually, of course, he founded the 1,500-store J.C. Penney chain.

Elected to the Baseball Hall of Fame in 1995, with the largest number of votes ever cast for one player, Mick Schmidt hit more home runs than any other major league third baseman, won three National League most valuable player awards and ten Gold Gloves. Schmidt, who played his whole eighteen-year career for the Philadelphia Phillies, does not want his achievements to be taken for granted. "The greatest misconceptions are that it probably came easy, that I didn't work very hard," he said. "But if time and effort were measured by the amount of dirt on your uniform, mine would have been black. You would never have been able to see the numbers. "

"Working hard becomes a habit, a serious kind of fun. You get self-satisfaction from pushing yourself to the limit, knowing that all the effort is going to pay off." Mary Lou Retton, Olympic gold medal gymnast

---

Jonathan Dolgen, chairman of Viacom Entertainment Group, described his work day: "You come to work in the morning...and you work twelve hours, and then you're off twelve hours. And then you come to work again, and you push, and keep pushing, and learn, and keep learning. And you begin to accomplish what you want...The trick is tenacity."

"It takes five years of very hard work to become an instant success." William Shea Jr.

———

The name of Thomas Alva Edison is synonymous with invention. By the end of his life there were 1,093 patents in his name, including those for the electric light bulb, the carbon-resistance telephone transmitter, the phonograph, and the first fully effective movie camera. Referring to his own lifetime of achievement, Edison once said, "I never did anything worth doing by accident, nor did any of my inventions come by accident; they came by work."

———

"I see myself as a doer. I'm sure that other people have had ideas that were similar to mine. The difference is that I have carried mine into action, and they have not." Nolan Bushnell, founder, Atari Computer Co.

———

"Opportunities are usually disguised as hard work, so most people don't recognize them." Ann Landers, syndicated columnist

What you said about
HARD WORK

❦

Hard work is a virtue that is important to this company in order to keep a competitive edge in a tough industry.

MARK LEVY
Vice President, MBNA Information Service, Inc.

We believe that more often than not hard work is the key to success. Through extra effort, intelligent people can overcome most obstacles.

JOSEPH GRANT
Executive Financial Officer, EDS

TOWARD VIRTUOSITY

❦

It's easy to tell how hard your body is running by taking your pulse or noting how out of breath you get. But how do you measure how hard you work at your job? You can't measure only in hours, can you?

Just for one week, try being the first one in the office in the morning and the last one to leave at night.

Do you waste a lot of time worrying over how long a project will take? Give yourself a time limit. Knowing you *have* to stop at a certain point actually makes you more productive. Or try plunging into an onerous task for a very short time. Gradually increase the period. It's painless and it really works. Soon you'll be able to work for three times as long as before.

———

Make a list of nonrequired work activities that will help you in the long run. Get at least one article published per year that will garner recognition in your field. Speak at a convention. Attend a seminar. Lead an off-the-record product development huddle.

———

Do you procrastinate? What percentage of your time at work is spent at lunch, on personal calls, or zoning out between tasks?

INITIATIVE

S enior executives fall into three
categories: those who make things happen;
those who watch things happen; and those
who wonder what happened.

*T*he best job for an employee who constantly says, "Because that's the way we've always done it," is with the competition.

Sam Walton didn't become the billionaire founder of Wal-Mart by sitting around waiting for others to tell him what to do. In the late 1950s, he owned a tiny chain of general merchandise stores in the south. As the hula hoop craze swept the nation, he couldn't keep enough in stock to satisfy his customers' demand. Did he watch all that profit go rolling away? No sirree bob. He ordered some plastic tubing and made his own hula hoops—three thousand of them a night!

Proactive is the opposite of reactive. Proactive people anticipate problems and opportunities and respond to them.

When Ann Winkleman Brown took over the helm at the Consumer Product Safety Commission, which had been described as "moribund" and "dormant" by consumer advocates, she too complained the agency was "all bun and no beef. They never took an action." Her goal: to turn the CPSC into "an activist agency." She demanded action and progress on every issue—warnings released, press conferences convened, safe-product awards granted, government delays avoided. No less a personage than Ralph Nader has credited Brown with having resuscitated the commission.

In *The Seven Habits of Highly Effective People*, Stephen Covey described taking initiative as "recognizing our responsibility to make things happen. Many people wait for something to happen or someone to take care of them. But people who end up with the good jobs are the proactive ones who are solutions to problems, not problems themselves, who seize the initiative to do whatever is necessary, consistent with correct principles, to get the job done." Covey continued, "The difference between people who exercise initiative and those who don't is literally the difference between night and day. I'm not talking about a 25 to 50 percent difference in effectiveness; I'm talking about a 5,000-plus percent difference, particularly if they are smart, aware, and sensitive to others."

———

One perceptive company president realized his customers were not as satisfied as they could be because none of his customer service representatives were taking any initiative. For example, the company had recently instituted a policy not to accept checks; yet when the president asked the accounting department how many checks had been returned in the last five years, the answer was *one*. The company president decided to have a retreat for his customer contact employees to explore how they could change. Turned out the people on the front lines had done a lot of thinking about how to do a better job, and came up with lots of examples of policies that made it difficult to provide the best service for customers. But, as at many corporations, the employees were afraid of making mistakes and weren't comfortable taking initiative. For the next six months, management never criticized the customer service people. All of a sudden, recalled the president, "our people on the phone began to make their own decisions on the spot, instead of passing the customer around. That resulted in much happier customers and increased business."

———

Sometimes a little initiative can save a company big money. The founder of her own company recalled starting out in business with a summer job answering toll-free calls from Triple A Club members. Often, she'd get calls that were for other Triple A offices, and was frustrated that she couldn't provide the information they needed. So the enterprising young employee checked her own Triple A card. It read: *In Virginia, call 1-800-234-6573*. Callers thought that meant if you wanted reservations in Virginia you should use that number. The young employee went right to the president with her interpretation. Triple A changed all the cards to read "from Virginia" instead of "in Virginia," and saved about $80,000.

What you said about INITIATIVE

Fifteen percent of survey respondents believe being proactive or showing initiative is essential to any business success.

> *Proactive means that you have employees who are actively thinking about the customer and the business. The more employees you have doing this the better you will serve the customer and the more opportunities you will be able to capitalize on.*
>
> GREGORY ZOBEL
> COO, Bay Brook Medical Services

> *Seizing the initiative can make all the difference between winning and losing.*
>
> THOMAS DAVIS III
> Vice President, Human Resources, BJ's Wholesale Club

We desperately need people who not only recognize the need to continuously improve, but also step forward to direct the changes that inevitably lead to those improvements.

MICHAEL BRAGG
Vice President, State Farm Insurance Company

Proactive = in favor of action. Opposite of reaction in response to stimulus. Old "wait-and-see, comparative analysis, measured response" is anachronistic given the times. Got to stay out ahead.

LINDA DOVE
Administrator, Ernst & Young

TOWARD VIRTUOSITY

Listen to yourself speaking, both out loud and internally, for one day. How often do you use phrases such as "If only," "I can't," or "There's nothing I can do about that"?

Now, for one day, practice substituting "I will," "I choose," and "I'm going to look at alternatives." Can you hear the difference? Do you notice the difference in your own actions?

Make a list of ten actions you could take at work that aren't part of your job description but that would contribute something positive.

Reading this book took initiative. How else have you taken initiative lately?

INTEGRITY

There's a big difference between
unnecessary or tactless honesty and
business integrity. Integrity is treating
people and organizations the way
you'd like to be treated.

A new manager at Procter & Gamble was asked by her intimidating boss to index some numbers for a business plan. She had no experience in dealing with mathematical projections, and was afraid to confess her lack of experience. "I had no idea what he meant. If I asked for his help, he'd know I was stupid, but I wasn't willing to spend the rest of my career covering up. So I said, 'Okay, I'm sorry, give me some help.'" Since then, Skye Hallberg has started her own company. Perhaps one reason for its amazing success is that she insists her employees be equally honest about their ignorance.

"Honesty is the cornerstone of all success, without which confidence and ability to perform shall cease to exist." Mary Kay Ash, CEO, Mary Kay Cosmetics

---

Lee Iacocca was CEO when Chrysler became involved in a scandal involving turning back the mileage on executive demo cars. He stood up in front of the press the next day and admitted that Chrysler was wrong, that their behavior was dishonest. Within a day, the scandal was over.

One day fashion designer Donna Karan dropped cigarette ash on the chenille DKNY sweater she was wearing. It burst into flame, and although she was unscathed, she immediately ordered every sweater from every store recalled. The next day Barbra Streisand called asking whether Karan could help her locate the same chenille sweater. It just about killed her to say no to her longtime idol, but Karan told the truth.

Harriet Craig Peterson, President of Cornerstone International Group, shared this tale of virtues in the international workplace: "I have been working in Russia and the former Soviet Union for the past four years. In one of my initial negotiation sessions, I had agreed upon the price of a product with the supplier, in this case popcorn to be grown under contract by Russian farmers. Based on this agreement price, I shipped hybrid popcorn seed to Russia, engaged the services of an agronomy consultant, developed test plots for planting various varieties of seed, and laid out the test plots for planting. When I arrived in town to sign the contract, the farm director mentioned that we had not completed our negotiation on price. To my amazement, he requested a price 700 percent higher than that originally agreed to. After four hours of negotiating, they were at 500 percent over our previously agreed upon price. In disgust, I threw my briefcase on the table, declared that their negotiations were "highway robbery" and stormed out. They followed me to the car, further lowering their price, but still not within the realm of reality. What did I learn from this experience? In Russia, a contract is not complete (and can be renegotiated) until the ink is dry on the signatures. They were not cheating and taking advantage of me; they were working according to their business culture."

———

The president of Connecticut College, Claire L. Gaudiani, believes the very nature of democracy in this country is at risk because "honesty is the civic virtue ignored by the insurance cheaters, the Wall Street trickster-traders, the Medicare-defrauding doctors and a host of other miscreants in white and blue collars."

———

A very successful entrepreneur still remembers her first boss. He would put receipts for personal items in the petty cash drawer, thereby cheating the company. "It colored my whole attitude toward him. I felt I could never trust him."

What you said about
INTEGRITY

Honesty and integrity—and by inference, trustworthiness—were among the most cited virtues, scoring on more than one third of the surveys received nationwide.

I need to hear the good and bad news to manage. We all make mistakes, therefore we need to be honest and admit it.

J. B. FRITH
CEO, Metro Health Center

I am an investment manager. Given the notoriety of improper conduct by managers in the derivatives area, I think honesty is an essential virtue for survival in this business.

JAY HARBECK,
Vice President, Merrill Lynch Asset Management

Honesty saves us time in looking for hidden agendas.

STEVE RUFFINO
Partner, Gibney Anthony

As Ross Perot said about an American politician, "If your wife can't trust you, why should I?" Trust is the cornerstone of all American business relationships and international relationships.

JOHN DUNN
President, J. H. Dunn and Company

If a person is not honest you never know what the facts are, can never fix a problem, just don't know where you really are. I can't deal with this!!!

ALAN MILLER
President and CEO, Universal Health Services, Inc.

You don't need to "look over your shoulder" or be concerned about the statement if your person is honest.

ROBERT GALECKE
Principal, Pate Winters and Stone

If you can't be honest, you might as well cash it in.

KEVIN LAWYER
Vice President Human Resources, Immunologic Pharmaceutical Corp.

If we are not honest with our constituents (customers, employees, bosses, shareholders, and regulators) we can never gain creditability regardless of our achievements.

KK DOMINGOS III
Senior Executive Vice President, Hibernia National Bank

Honesty is the first word in the dictionary of virtues.

JOE FORTSON
Parvest Capital Group

If you start dealing with facts, rather than half truths or lies, you save time and make more money.

RONALD PAGE
Vice President, A. G. Edwards

TOWARD VIRTUOSITY

You cannot be honest with the rest of the world unless you are honest with yourself. Write down an honest appraisal of yourself as an employee and as a supervisor. Ask someone you trust for feedback. How honest were you?

What's your company's standard for honesty and integrity? Do your employees know exactly where you draw the line?

How far are you willing to bend? Situational ethics are the downfall of countless politicians and executives. Decide *before* temptation occurs exactly what you're willing to do—and not do.

Talk on the phone as if it were tapped by your boss and your employees. Treat the letters and e-mail you write the same way. It's a lot easier to keep your stories straight, when your public and private versions of the truth match.

INTELLIGENCE

Some people are born smart, but
*intelligence is acquired. You can't be
intelligent without knowledge,
and knowledge comes from research,
education, and access to data.*

*I*gnorance is not a simple lack of knowledge, according to British philosopher Karl Popper's theory, but an active aversion to knowledge, the refusal to know, issuing from cowardice, pride, or laziness of mind. In Popper's philosophy, ignorance has an ethical dimension, and *knowing* is a moral obligation for human beings.

———

"A man should keep his little brain attic stocked with all the furniture that he is likely to use, and the rest he can put away in the lumber room of his library, where he can get it if he wants it." Sherlock Holmes

———

Peter Russell wrote in *The Brain Book* that "Immediate memory is limited to about seven 'chunks' of information. Most people can remember about seven numbers in a row, seven colors, seven shapes, or seven of any other item. So if you need to remember more than seven items, it's better to organize them into a smaller number of chunks."

———

Successful business leaders rarely use erudite references to phenomenology, Gödel's theorem, or nuclear fusion to impress clients. Instead, they focus on the strategies, tactics, facts, and figures of their business. By focusing creative energy on a sliver of *all* knowledge, they're able to maximize their *business intelligence*.

———

"Knowledge and human power are synonymous, since the ignorance of the first frustrates the effect." Francis Bacon, 1561–1626, Lord Chancellor of England

Tom Wilson, a salesman for a leading software company, always seemed on the ball about his prospect's stores. A colleague asked him how he got to be so smart about the retailing business. "The secret," he said, "is to read their annual report before you go on a sales call. The concerns of the CEO always manage to filter down to the buyers, so if you know what you're up against, you can address it."

———

Most people would rather *talk* to a smart person than *listen* to one. One of the most effective ways to demonstrate your intelligence is by keeping your mouth shut, listening carefully, and then integrating critical elements of the other person's ideas in your own analysis.

What you said about INTELLIGENCE

Intelligence ranked number five among the virtues. More than a quarter of survey respondents said it was a key business trait.

———

> *If an individual has the intellect, it is highly probable that he can deal with development needs to correct areas of personal weakness.*
>
> E. ALAN ERB
> President, Brown Products

———

*The best and the brightest are the best people to hire.
Challenge them, let them run with the ball a little—you get
great results!*

> JOHN SHAKER
> Senior Vice President Licensing, BMI

---

*Intelligence is fundamental to executing our business. People
with all other characteristics will still fail if they are not
"above average" in intelligence.*

> JACK ROBERTS
> Senior Managing Director, Bear, Stearns & Co.

---

*The best athlete can play any sport . The intelligent
employee/co-worker can learn, adapt, and contribute.*

> STEVE KAPLAN
> President, Kaplan & Co.

TOWARD VIRTUOSITY

What are the hardest questions facing your division and your
industry? Write them down. Just identifying problems is a big
first step toward solving them.

Read. And read some more. Reading is the single most effective way to gain knowledge, which turns into intelligence.
Does your company allow you to expense books you purchase?
Try visiting the bookstore at least once a month. Since the
average American buys just *one* book a year, you'll have an
almost unfair advantage!

Make the most of the intelligence you already possess by taking care of your body. That includes eating high protein, low fat foods; working under full spectrum light; getting enough sleep and exercise; and avoiding too much alcohol, caffeine, and other "substances."

Part of being smart involves knowing when to admit you don't know something. The brightest people ask the most questions. If you don't know, ask.

The informational interview isn't just for job seekers. Find experts in your field and take them to lunch. Pick their brains, then pick up the check.

LEADERSHIP

E xecutive director Mitzi Sales looks
for employees who take responsibility
for their own actions. Otherwise, she says,
they don't have the leadership qualities or
willingness to take on new projects,
do something a new way, lead other
people along a new path.

Writer and scholar Warren G. Bennis once said, "The first job of a leader is to define a vision for the organization...but without longevity of leadership you can have the 'vision of the month club.' Leadership is the capacity to translate vision into reality."

Leadership is an action, not a position.

"The number one leadership skill is the ability to develop others," writes Tom Peters. "That's not a new idea. But, boss, check your calendar: How much time are you devoting directly to people-development? One colleague at Apple Computer formally dedicates one hundred days a year to what, with a smile, he calls 'performance reviews.' Twenty-five people report to him, and twice a year they spend two days, one on one, reviewing where they've been together and where they're going next. Talk about putting your calendar where your mouth is! "

"We have to undo a one hundred-year-old concept and convince our managers that their role is not to control people and stay 'on top' of things, but rather to guide, energize and excite." Jack Welch, CEO, General Electric

---

Peter Flynn, an NBC executive, said Grant Tinker was a leader with a tremendous ability to share the credit, give others autonomy, and pick the right employees. Flynn continued, "We were always breaking our necks for him because he created a real sense of unity. He had a huge sense of what we could do. He would pick the best people he could from the creative community and then just let them work. Even if a program wasn't getting good ratings, he'd leave it there and let viewers find it. He had a lot of faith in people. It paid off. NBC was number one for nine years."

————

Carol Caruthers, the national director of financial planning at Price Waterhouse, says that among the most important lessons she has learned as a manager, is where to focus her energies. "My vice chairman said to me one day, 'Do you put most of your time in the people you can count on or the people who are letting you down?' Caruthers realized she was spending too much time on the nonproductive people. "You better put 80 percent of your time on your best people," the vice chairman told her. "Tell the others you'll help them, too, when they turn themselves around."

————

"I cannot do what most of my employees can do, and I'm pleased to let them know it by showing respect for the jobs they do. If I do know how to do their job, I keep that to myself. I want them to feel I'm dependent on them." Judith Ann Eigen, President, Judith Ann Creations, Inc.

————

At one point in his career as a marine, Lieutenant Joseph Gorman was on a ship headed toward Lebanon. Although he cannot remember exactly how long the trip was (he estimated ten to twelve days at sea), one memory that sticks out in his mind is the moment his superior pulled him aside to remind him that his most important mission wasn't in Lebanon, but right there on the ship. He needed to gain control and earn respect from his troops. From that day on, Joseph Gorman made leadership his number one priority, stressing trust and teamwork as necessities as well. He has been rewarded for this behavior: recently, he was appointed chairman of the Marine Scholarship Fund.

————

"It is commitment, not authority, that produces results."
William L. Gore, founder and CEO, W. L. Gore & Associates

Skye Hallberg, who runs her own company, makes a point of taking any potential employee out for a drive. "If people drive watching the bumper in front of them, that's how they run their business lives. I like people who are looking at the road ahead, who can anticipate. I read a study of leadership where they tried to figure out a single commonality. It wasn't a question of intellect, it was ability to anticipate results of actions."

"A leader is a dealer in hope." Napoleon Bonaparte, 1769–1821

In the book *21st Century Leadership*, William Solomon writes, "There has been a massive change in corporate leadership in the last fifteen to twenty years. Leadership and a sense of accountability for what really goes on in the organization have been pushed down and distributed throughout the organization."

What you said about
LEADERSHIP

Change is so difficult that above all I believe we need leaders at all levels who can stay focused while learning, adapting, and bringing long term results.

F. HANCKEL
COO, Long Beach Memorial Hospital

Leader—you have to be looking out the windshield, not the rear view mirror, to go forward.

JAMES TAYLOR
Executive Director, Christie Clinic Association

Leadership is the foundation upon which business must rely to grow or it will fail. There is no substitute. The leader must be the teacher.

W. H. PARKER
President, Parker Sales Co.

An outstanding leader exhibits many of the virtues listed above. If the CEO lacks leadership, nothing will be accomplished.

ARCHIE DUNHAM
Executive Vice President, Conoco Inc.

TOWARD VIRTUOSITY

Who are the leaders you follow? Why do you follow them?

Have you had a boss who didn't know how to lead? What attributes made him hard to follow?

Does your company reward leaders? How?

In the last year, how many times have you acted as a leader and had people follow you? Make a list of five or six situations and see what they have in common.

LOYALTY

Courtesy, honesty and loyalty to its *staff paid off in many ways for a growing airline from the South. Delta Airlines treated its employees so well that they responded by buying the airline a jet.*

*L*oyalty is a two-way virtue. A corporation trusts its employees to stay loyal, and employees trust the company to treat them well. Unfortunately, in the face of today's downsizings, a loyalty gap has opened up, according to Roper Reports. More Americans say they feel a great deal of loyalty to their job than think their employers feel a great deal of loyalty toward them. Survey responses: Loyal to my company: 47 percent. My company is loyal to me: 32 percent.

When your company hired you, they took a chance. They promised to pay you and let you learn, and they hoped that you'd produce. You owe your company the same chance at the end of your career with them. If you've found a better situation, or if your current situation isn't working, you owe it to your boss to give him/her a chance to fix it.

"An ounce of loyalty is worth a pound of cleverness." Elbert Hubbard, American writer, printer, and editor

---

John Capozzi tells the following remarkable story of loyalty in his book, *Why Climb the Corporate Ladder When You Can Take the Elevator?*: "I was involved in several business deals with a fellow from Santa Barbara, California. He was a likable guy, but his luck in business was awful. Although he built up some success, he financed a large business in 1983 and lost $10 million—just about his entire net worth at the time. The result of this loss was terrible on him. He became increasingly depressed and, at the bottom, attempted suicide. I found out about his situation through a mutual friend. I then called Ray Chambers, another friend who also knew him well. Ray was the founder and chairman of Wesray at the time, and agreed to help. Two days later, Ray and I flew to Santa Barbara on Ray's private jet. Ray lent him $150,000 and I lent him $75,000, to get him on his feet and started again. Over the years, our mutual friend has continued to struggle, trying to regain his fortunes. Neither Ray nor I have ever been paid back in actual cash. Instead, the fellow we helped has introduced me to some wonderful people; since 1983 I've easily earned ten times the amount I lent him, from the contacts I've met."

———

It's not a matter of loyalty if you go to work every day because you can't find a better job—that's self-interest. Loyalty is the ability to do something that is not in your immediate best interest as a way of furthering a person, a cause, or a company you believe in. Captured spies who won't betray secrets, or husbands who won't write juicy biographies of famous wives are loyal.

———

"In politics, loyalty is everything." James Eastland, late U.S. Senator

———

The consummate Washington insider, House Speaker Tip O'Neill was always loyal to his Boston constituents. He followed his axiom "All politics is local" because it got him reelected, and he also did it because he believed he owed it to the people who put him in office.

———

Rosemary Woods, the late President Richard Nixon's secretary, never revealed what happened to the eighteen minutes on the tapes. Even though she could have reaped huge personal profits, and avoided subpoenas and harassment, Woods showed her loyalty to her boss, the Commander in Chief. Whatever you think of Nixon and his acts, he had to be pleased by the loyalty shown by this member of his staff.

———

"The manager who supports the boss—the manager whom the boss can rely on and trust—is the one who will be given the most freedom and the least supervision." Mary Ann and Eric Allison, *Managing Up, Managing Down*

What you said about
LOYALTY

I believe loyalty to be the most important virtue because the individual will always do his/her very best job.

GENEVIEVE RYAN
President, Business Capital Group

Loyalty—there is no substitute. Give me loyal employees and we will build a great company.

STEPHEN COLLINS
Vice President Membership, VHA

Loyalty is a two-way street. If you and your company are truly loyal, it's a guarantee that employees will be the same.

JOHN MCAULIFFE
President, John T. McAuliffe Sales Co.

TOWARD VIRTUOSITY

Is your strongest loyalty to your family? Your country? Your company? Your religion? How far are you willing to go to be loyal?

Are you earning loyalty from co-workers and others? What have you done to earn it?

Blind loyalty does no one or company much good. Know who and what your loyalty stands for.

Loyalty is more than showing up at a job. Do you badmouth your company to others? Share company secrets? Act in a selfish way instead of for the good of the group?

One of the best ways to generate loyalty is to offer it. If you stick with your employees, or your boss, through hard times, that feeling is far more likely to be reciprocated.

PERSISTENCE

Winston Churchill, asked to give a *graduation speech at Oxford University, stepped up to the podium and said, "Never, never, never give up." Then he sat down.*

*H*ank Aaron struck out more often than almost any other player, and amazingly enough, never led the league in single season home runs. But through sheer persistence, he broke Babe Ruth's record of 713 home runs.

Ken Tuchman started out in business by importing Philippine puka shells used in necklaces surfers wore. By age fifteen, he was one of the country's largest puka shell importers, with customers such as J.C. Penney and Pier I Imports. By seventeen, he had founded three other small businesses. Next, he started Teletech, a centralized calling center, with $250,000 in bank loans. Ken was off to a faster start than most entrepreneurs. However, in 1986, an accounting firm told him he was technically bankrupt. Rather than cutting his losses and giving up, Tuchman persisted in believing that the company was onto something big. Teletech revenues in 1994 were $38 million and he plans to open three more call centers this year.

"People can smell emotional commitment (and the absence thereof) from a mile away. When I was in a relatively junior job in and around the White House, I seemed to get an inordinate amount done (that's what people said, anyway, which is what counts). The secret was my bulldog-like persistence on issues that mattered to me—I'd wear the bastards down. That was about it. The bastards had their own agendas, and the things I was working on usually weren't at the top of them. Given my tenacity, they'd usually let me have my way rather than waste a lot of time fighting." Tom Peters, best-selling author

---

Sunkist Growers, the orange cooperative, has had a long, successful history exporting fruit to Japan. The company has even developed great relationships with Japan's often touchy farmers. How did Sunkist succeed where so many other exporters have failed? The head of the company visited Japan regularly for more than thirty years. He didn't have a short term agenda—sometimes even his long term goals weren't obvious. He was the tortoise, not the hare, and by persisting, he developed contacts and most of all, trust.

———

Thomas Edison insisted that he wasn't a brilliant inventor. When faced with a problem, he merely tried every conceivable solution until he found one. He even tried using human hair as a filament for the light bulb. In fact, he tried to invent a light bulb more than one thousand times before succeeding. Yet asked how it felt to have failed so often, Edison demonstrated the attitude that ultimately led to his achievement: "I have not failed. I've discovered one thousand ways not to build a light bulb."

———

Mountain climbers are testimony to the power of persistence. Even Mount Everest can be climbed, as long as you concentrate on taking one step at a time and don't stop until you get to the top.

———

If one out of ten sales calls leads to new business, a pessimist would call that a 10 percent success rate. A successful salesperson realizes that all he has to do is be turned down nine times before he's virtually guaranteed a sale. By viewing rejection as a stepping stone to acceptance, salespeople are able to persist until they achieve their goals.

What you said about
PERSISTENCE

Rejection and defeat can only be overcome with persistence.

KEN DIEKROEGER
Principal, The Shansby Group

Persistence has extreme value in today's business climate. Without the ability to take one more shot at a problem, try a new approach, or modify the status quo, we don't move forward and good ideas go unfulfilled.

M. SCHNEIDER
Vice President, Systems Integration, Interim Services

At the end of the day, it's tenacity which makes winners of those who weather the short-term ups and downs to accomplish goals, scale mountains.

JOHN GRACE
Senior Vice President, Gerstman & Meyers Inc.

Never say never when a real opportunity to make a good business deal is on the table.

MIKE CARRANCEJIE
Executive Vice President, Joe Foster Company

TOWARD VIRTUOSITY

Is there a tradition of persistence in your company? Are there legends or heroes who have paved the way for you to persist?

Rank yourself: on a scale of one to ten, how likely are you to stick with a project instead of giving up? How do those you admire rate when it comes to persistence?

Keep track of your successes. Make a list of ten instances when you felt like quitting but persisted instead—and succeeded. Then, the next time you're facing a seemingly insurmountable task, read your list to remind yourself of your ability to persist and triumph.

The number one enemy of persistence is procrastination. Try keeping a log of the projects you're working on to make sure you're spending enough time on projects that need you most, not just the easy ones.

RESOURCEFULNESS

Why do some succeed where others *have failed? All other things being equal, the difference between success and failure is simple resourcefulness: Maximizing the value of what you already have.*

*M*ickey Mouse began his life as a silent cartoon character. But by the time Walt Disney had finished creating his first Mickey films, sound had become so popular that no one would buy a speechless Mickey. Walt, who was completely broke, told his brother Roy, "Don't worry. I'll just add sound." So, using his own, cost-free voice, Disney turned the mouse into the talking cash cow that we all know and love today.

"Take control of your own self-development," said William F. Jackson, vice president of Development Dimensions International, a personnel assessment firm. "Don't assume that the organization will provide you with clearly designed career paths and carefully crafted developmental experiences."

One year a small but popular theater company had a severe cash flow problem. When the set designer asked the business manager for his budget on *Father's Day*, the play they were producing, she said, "Zero. Any dollar you spend will be over budget. We're in dire straits. Do what you can." So the set designer went to a bike shop, got lots of cardboard boxes, and actually carved furniture out of cardboard. "It was extraordinary, one of the best sets we ever had," recalled the business manager, "and truly resourceful."

Rebecca Cole has built her business from being resourceful. She is a recycling artist who finds great junk and turns it into gold. How? She plants beautiful little gardens in containers ranging from bathtubs to wooden drawers to children's suitcases. Then she sells them in her popular shop in New York City.

The judges at the 1994 International Design Fair in Nagaoka, Japan, chose fifty-seven winners from a field of six hundred entries. Among the winners was Dwight Huffman, twenty-seven, of Ithaca, New York. Huffman's resourceful furniture is made of salvaged wooden pallets discarded from loading docks. His five-pound stackable bistro chair has an aluminum frame and oak and cherrywood slats, an overlooked resource.

What you said about
RESOURCEFULNESS

Resourceful: In small- and medium-sized companies you don't always have the support in-house to accomplish what you need to do. It's vital to be able to see different ways to reach a goal.

LORRIANE MONTHEIR
Director of Administration, Phelan, Pope, Cahill & Devine Ltd.

A resourceful person will find the answer, or find the necessary contact; you don't have to hold their hand and it's much more productive.

CANDACE ALCORN
Senior Vice President Marketing, Snelling & Snelling

As an attorney, I come up against diverse issues and challenges that require immediate responses. Therefore, I need my paralegal assistants to be resourceful.

K. NEWBOLD
Partner, Tedder, Blake, Newbold

Our employees' resourcefulness has increased productivity by 139 percent where staff was reduced by 25 percent.

ELAINE GRESS
Vice President Administration, National Motor Club of America

---

Many employees are asked to contribute more to their companies than in the past; it is essential that employees be resourceful to find creative/quick solutions.

H.A. VILLAREAL
Vice President Human Resources, Cadbury Beverages

With ever-changing job responsibilities, the ability to get the right resources to get the job done is critical.

DOROTHY ROACH
World Wide Controller, Alcoa

Resourceful managers are capable of improving productivity even with severe budget cuts, which results in doing more with the same or fewer resources.

C. LEE JONES
President, Linda Hall Library

Many times when confronted with new or challenging problems, knowing whom to call or where to go for the answers is a valuable tool.

MARK BOYD
Senior Human Resources Specialist, Hitachi Semiconductor

We compete with large multinational corporations. To be effective and produce expected bottom line results, our group must have high energy and be very resourceful in their selling efforts.

THOMAS BRIGGS
President, B-Line Systems

TOWARD VIRTUOSITY

On a scale of one to ten, how resourceful are you? Are you more likely to spend time thinking of excuses or solutions?

Try this exercise: imagine ten different uses for a metal bucket.

List all the resources, both external and internal, that you have at your disposal. Take your time, and write them down. You'll be surprised.

Can you remember a difficult work situation that you feel you didn't handle as effectively as you wished? Now redo that moment mentally. What resources could you bring to bear that would change the outcome?

RESPONSIBILITY

Successful individuals assume
responsibility. They have internalized
President Truman's motto:
The Buck Stops Here.

An engineer who has worked at AT&T for more than twenty years said he tries to take engineering courses, although his work schedule often doesn't permit him that luxury. "If I think I need to learn more about power circuits, and my boss says no, he really needs me now, it's still my responsibility. I'll take the course at night or on weekends. It's my problem."

If you owned the company where you work, would you behave differently? That's one definition of responsibility.

Being slow to take responsibility cost Intel more than a billion dollars when the Pentium scandal blew. Bear Stearns financial analyst Andrew Neff analyzed the corporate behavior regarding the chip this way: "Intel acted like Mr. Spock; they should have acted like Captain Kirk. I think that people wanted Intel to admit that they were wrong."

Gordon Segal, founder of Crate and Barrel, has a knack for keeping his thousands of employees striving for excellence while working in retail—not an atmosphere known for making employees feel appreciated. In a recent interview he explained, "We make each salesperson the head of a department in the store—the kitchenware area or the glassware area, for example—within a couple of months. So let's say a typical Crate and Barrel is 8,000 square feet, and we have about six or seven department heads. Each one manages about 1,200 feet; it's like their own little store. The department heads are responsible not only for maintaining the displays and keeping inventories, but also for educating their customers and conducting meetings on their products. They're generally responsible for how well the department does. We take young people and make them merchants early on. We don't say, 'You're a salesclerk for the next two or three years, then if you're okay, we'll give you some other job.' We give them a lot of responsibility so they feel very fulfilled and challenged."

In *The Joy of Working*, Denis Waitley and Reni Witt wrote: "When you take responsibility for your thoughts, your work habits, your goals, your life, you'll find you're creating your own horoscope for success. Once you sow the seeds—being true to yourself, taking control, and accepting responsibility—you'll reap a harvest of fulfillment and joy."

Nordstrom, home of legendary customer service (and regular profits), has condensed its entire employee handbook into one sentence: *Use your best judgment.* By insisting that employees with direct customer contact take responsibility for the store's image and relationship with customers, Nordstrom has created a culture of responsibility.

More often than not, individuals are not given responsibility. They *take* it.

What you said about
RESPONSIBILITY

*We are a very lean company spread out over three conti-
nents. We don't have the luxury of looking over others'
shoulders. Each and every one of us must take responsibility
for our actions, or we let the whole company down.*

PHILIP JOHNSON
Vice President Personnel and Administration, Equator USA Inc.

---

*In a societal culture which seems to allow avoidance of
responsibility and accountability, it is even more important
to hire individuals who take responsibility for themselves
and their actions. Employees who accept responsibility tend
to understand how their function fits within the organization, tend to be highly productive, and tend to be focused. In
my experience, responsible employees also are loyal, conscien-
tious, hard-working, and self-motivated.*

JAMES NOVELL
Executive Vice President, Crozer-Keystone Health System

---

*In today's work environment, it is essential for individuals
to be "responsible" for their actions. The excuse "it's not my
job" just doesn't work anymore.*

BOB KAMMER
Human Resources Manager, Sanden International USA Inc.

Responsible, although less lofty than many of the choices, embodies the soul of an organization if the organization has a soul.

FRED LAQUINTO
Director Human Resources, Hercules

If a person is responsible, most other virtues follow.

DIANE FOUNTAIN
Campus Mail Coordinator, Cornell College

TOWARD VIRTUOSITY

The most difficult part of freedom is that everything is up to you. Were you late for work? Is the way you treated that client something you're proud of? Do you make enough money? Is your education and training the state-of-the-art? If you take control of your life, and take responsibility for all of your actions, your life will change.

List all the areas you are directly responsible for at work. Do you feel you really are responsible in these areas? Do you avoid making excuses, whining, or blaming others?

Who is the most responsible person you know? What makes him or her seem so responsible?

Think about people you have to hire, from babysitters to house painters to secretaries: how do you judge them on responsibility? Would you pass your own test?

SELF-
MOTIVATION

All motivation is self-motivation.
Your family, your boss or your co-workers
can try to get your engine going, but until you
decide what to accomplish,
nothing will happen.

*I*van G. Seidenberg started at NYNEX right out of high school as an assistant for telephone repairmen. Seidenberg put himself through college at night, then got his master's degree in business administration, all while working at NYNEX. Finally, after twenty-eight years of self-motivation, he was named chairman and chief executive of the NYNEX Corporation, at age forty-seven. The company had $12 billion in revenues last year.

———

In *Why Climb the Corporate Ladder When You Can Take the Elevator?*, John Capozzi writes: "The day I started as a ticket agent I also started my own promotion plan. This plan has served me well for my entire business career. In essence, the plan was simple, although in execution it required extra work on a daily basis. The plan was to immediately select the next job I wanted. I then set out to learn to do that job as well as the person currently holding the position. When the job became available, I was known to be more qualified than any of the other candidates."

———

After his grandfather refused to teach him the awning business, claiming it was dying, Maxwell Eaton started his own awning manufacturing company called Otter Creek Industries. He sold his boat and car to start the business and began creating canvas bags to sell to commercial establishments. Within a year, he landed a job creating an awning for a local ski resort. Within months, he had even more takers. Eaton said his grandfather's advice was the best he's ever received. By going it alone, Eaton has carved his own million-dollar niche in the awning manufacturing industry — and proven the power of self-motivation.

———

"Let this be your motto—Rely on yourself! For, whenever the prize be a ribbon or a throne, the victor is he who can get it alone!" John Godfrey Saxe, 1818–1887, American newspaper publisher and editor

According to entrepreneur Eric Twerdahl, the smaller the business, the more important self-motivation. "We're a mergers and acquisitions company," explained Twerdahl. "We had an overseas client who said he wanted to establish an offshore banking presence. That's all he told us. We could have dropped the ball because we didn't have enough information. But a colleague was sufficiently self-motivated that he investigated on his own, found out all the regulations, narrowed down locations, and presented the information to the client. The client was very happy, and our firm made a lot of money."

"The American system of ours, call it Americanism, call it Capitalism, call it what you like, gives each and every one of us a great opportunity if we only seize it with both hands and make the most of it," Al Capone, 1899–1947, American gangster

At age twenty-five, Didem Altop is the youngest of seventy-five consultants in the Washington office of EDS Management Consulting Services. The eldest child of Turkish immigrants, she grew up in Pittsburgh, earned her BA in international relations from Johns Hopkins, and so wanted a job at the World Bank that she was happy to work without pay.

Although bank administrators warned her not to, Altop listened to her own advice. "I thought if I could get my foot in the door I could establish my competence," she said. Within two months, Altop became a paid research analyst for Algeria and Morocco and traveled there every six weeks for over a year. She was one of the World Bank's first research analysts who didn't have, or wasn't working toward, a master's degree. Instead, she was working hard on self-motivation.

———————

Thousands of years ago, Plato wrote, "The man who makes everything that leads to happiness depend upon himself, and not other men, has adopted the very best plan for living happily."

What you said about SELF-MOTIVATION

Self-motivation made the top ten list of virtues in our survey. Twenty-two percent of executives checked it off.

This adds a dynamic atmosphere to an organization and also saves the entire organization time. In addition, self-motivated people also frequently generate new ideas.

LAWRENCE LEIGHTON
Managing Director, LM Capital

———————

External motivation is not as effective—don't have time to motivate.

TOM COOPER
CEO, Cooper Holding Corp.

———————

Self-motivated: There is, in any size organization, a propensity on the part of many to "get lost" in the process of accomplishment. I look for people who seek no excuses in getting things done.

FRANK GENCARELLI
Senior Vice President, First Colony Life

TOWARD VIRTUOSITY

Do you need a lot of outside feedback in order to get your job done? Or are you able to succeed because of the inner satisfaction you derive?

Try rewarding yourself, instead of waiting for others to reward you, for good work. Did you finish a project ahead of schedule? Beat your own sales record? Get a promotion? Take time out to celebrate your own achievements, to let them really register, before plowing into the next deadline or benchmark.

Do you wait for instructions?

List three areas in which you receive external recognition for a job well done. For example, maybe you get a year-end bonus for extra sales. Now think about how you could shift your focus from that monetary reward to inner motivation. Feel good about proving to yourself that you can top yourself.

Sense of
HUMOR

The sales director of a large New York corporation hired a theater director to teach his salesmen to smile. Sales went up 15 percent within three months of the lessons.

*C*omputer scientist Vinton Cerf is best known as the father of the Internet. He invented the Internet Protocol, the common language spoken by computers throughout the Internet. At a 1992 Internet Protocol meeting, a controversial issue had the engineers at one another's throats. Cerf took the podium to make some informal remarks. He then began to strip: first his coat, then his waistcoat, then his tie. Finally his shirt came off, revealing an undershirt that read "I P on Everything." The audience, of course, cracked up and all tension dissolved.

Jerry Seinfeld, everyone's favorite TV comedian, had a girl-friend who didn't laugh. He dumped her.

Ann Landers once said, "Don't accept your dog's admiration as conclusive evidence that you are wonderful."

Sun Microsystems thrives on a culture of wild creativity and off-the-wall thinking. At least once a year, engineers and executives band together to perform a dramatic prank; once, CEO Scott MacNeally found a Volkswagen Beetle parked in his office.

"What we are looking for first and foremost is a sense of humor," CEO Herb Kelleher told *Fortune* magazine. "Then we are looking for people who have to excel to satisfy themselves and who work well in a collegial environment. We don't care that much about education and experience, because we can train people to do whatever they have to do. We hire attitudes."

When interviewing potential employees, Mitzi Sales, executive director of a nonprofit agency, uses a strict congeniality test: if a person doesn't smile at least three times during the interview, Sales won't hire them. Why? "Because they're probably sour people, and in a teamwork situation you need pleasant people." Sales herself is known to "grin like an idiot throughout the entire interview." Perhaps the secret to her success...

"How much grief could be avoided if everyone at the workplace simply practiced a bit of consideration and courtesy!" Andrew S. Grove, CEO, Intel Corp.

One boss we know always answers the question, "How are you?" the same way. It doesn't matter if he has a bad cold, just lost a big account, and has to fire someone. When asked, he always says, "I'm just swell! How are you?" After saying this a few times, he often *does* feel swell.

Computer repairman: Has this system ever worked?
Office worker: No.
Computer repairman: Good. Now at least I know where to start.

What you said about SENSE OF HUMOR

Humor is a necessary business virtue because it engenders creativity, dispels anger, resentments, and hostility, reduces stress... and enables you to see yourself and your situation in the grand (and sometimes absurd) scheme of things.

DINA VON ZWECK
President, DVZ Inc.

*Phaedrus in the first century said it best: "You will break the
bow if you keep it always stretched."*

BOB LEVOY
President, Success Dynamics Inc.

---

*An individual without a sense of humor is almost impossi-
ble to work with or for—of limited intelligence—usually not
creative—in a word "Boring" to associates and clients.*

JOHN LYNCH III
Partner, Blackshaw, Olmstead & Lynch

TOWARD VIRTUOSITY

Don't confuse joking with a sense of humor. Jokes usually are
at someone or something's expense. A sense of humor has
more to do with being able to see the absurdity of a situation.
Even more important, a sense of humor implies being able to
laugh at oneself.

Make a point of laughing at yourself at least once a day.

Study the most successful people in your office. Do they smile
more often? Say hello more? Whatever they do is working, so
try to copy a few of their techniques. Soon you'll actually feel
more personable.

The next time you get angry at someone, stop before you
speak. Instead of sounding irritated, is there anything silly you
can say to diffuse the situation? Ms. Manners has one perfect

solution to rude, pesky people: no matter what they've said or done, just say, "How nice for you."

————

Do you think of yourself as someone with a sense of humor? Sometimes just switching the message playing inside your head can do wonders.

————

If you don't have the confidence to be verbally humorous, try surrounding yourself with things that will make you and others smile. Photographs of your favorite baby, funny toys, silly sculptures are props with personality.

Sense of
OWNERSHIP

Steve Jobs had the original members
*of the Macintosh team sign their names
on the computer's case. The first one
million Macintoshes went out the door with
those names engraved inside.*

*T*his virtue overlaps with responsibility. Employees with a sense of ownership take pride in their work, in the products they create, and in their company.

Harry Quadracci started one of the largest printing companies in this country, Quad/Graphics, Inc. According to Daniel Kehrer, author of *Doing Business Boldly*, much of Quad's phenomenal success has been the result of an Employee Stock Ownership Plan, ranked the best in the country. "Workers with high school educations or less are rapidly advanced to managers and encouraged to take risks immediately after they are indoctrinated," wrote Kehrer. Pressmen are called press managers at Quad. "If you are responsible for a $6 million press I have news for you," said Quadracci. "You're as much responsible for profits as I am." And a *Psychology Today* article described Quad's employees: "The workers act as though Quad's presses belong to them, because they do. They act as though every order is their personal responsibility, because it is."

For many years, France's Groupe Michelin held steadfastly to strict, inward-looking management systems that they considered essential for success. In the early '90s—when the company was suffering from a "too systematic approach" and its failure to modernize—the Michelin family realized they needed to reinvent the business by decentralizing and adopting innovative management techniques such as "empowering" employees by removing supervisors. Scary as these changes were to make, they resulted in an increase in productivity.

There are two definitions of employees with a sense of ownership, according to William Ferretti, Chairman and CEO of Medstar Communications, Inc.: one good and one bad. The man in the gray flannel suit who went to work in corporate America identified with the company, used the same phrases the boss used, had one sense of ownership, and was assured of job security. But now, Ferretti said, more employees are being encouraged to think for themselves, to be disagreeable. "Corporate America is even turning to the notion of employees evaluating their bosses. So thinking like owners means thinking for yourself. It's what the entrepreneur always thinks: what are we going to do to please the customers?"

An executive described how the CEO of Johnson & Johnson ignored the recommendations of his lawyers, financial people, and all his high-priced consultants after a few bottles of Tylenol were found to be tampered with. James Burke recalled every single Tylenol product. "He was thinking like an owner," said the executive, "of long term corporate reputation, not of his reputation as a CEO who would be blamed for ignoring his high paid consultant. Burke put himself in the shoes of the customer. He thought, 'If I'm a mother and use Tylenol, am I ever going to buy a Johnson product if I feel there's the slightest chance of playing Russian roulette with my child's well-being?' So he recalled every damn one of them, even though statistically there was no reason to. And I know I myself will never buy a pain reliever from anybody else as long as I live—because Burke thought of me, the customer."

What you said about
SENSE OF OWNERSHIP

Nearly 15 percent of survey respondents said this virtue was important.

Sense of ownership is key as it ensures workers will make decisions and act as if it was their own money. Furthermore, they will take responsibility to ensure work is done correctly, promptly and completely and others will take responsibility for their actions.

SAL AMATANGELO
Executive Vice President and CFO, The Upper Deck Company

Sense of ownership—employees must act in a caring fashion… that whatever they do it is as if it's their own money they are spending. Such an attitude assures time is not wasted, prudent risks are taken, and attention is paid to the bottom line.

MICHAEL JEANS
President, Wesson Peter Pan Foods Co.

Sense of ownership translates to "profit-oriented" in our company. Without profit, there is no business.

W. K. NELSON
Chairman and CEO, Nelson Communications Inc.

Weiss, Peck & Greer is an investment firm, therefore it is essential that the executives who run the companies we finance think like owners and not only as managers.

NORA KERPPOLA
Vice President, Weiss, Peck & Greer

The best people I have worked with at all levels treat their jobs and responsibilities as if they are owners of the whole business.

PETER HOWLEY
CEO, Howley Enterprises

In a small company it's imperative to have employees who have the belief that they are the "champion" of the work and projects they are responsible for.

STEPHEN ADLER
Vice President Human Resources, Sybron Chemicals Inc.

Sense of ownership—when a person can take full responsibility for his/her actions they will more likely make good choices and quickly earn the respect of their co-workers and customers. It is the basis from which other virtues stem.

MARY CAHILL
Customer Relations Manager, Infincom

Too many times, by far too many people, there is no sense of ownership in an individual product. Ownership brings pride in getting a job "well-done." This means a better result for everyone.

ROBERT KLEPPINGER
Vice President Claim Department, Prudential Reinsurance Company

TOWARD VIRTUOSITY

When you go to work, do you feel as if you're going to "their" office or to "our" office? Sometimes just a slight adjustment in attitude can yield big differences.

————

Does management fight against employees' natural tendency to take ownership for the work they create? Rotating assignments and too strict production manuals can kill any enthusiasm for making things better.

————

Make it a point to talk directly with the people who use the product or service you help create. If you're an inspector at General Motors, visit a few dealerships or talk to people as they visit the car wash. Give your ultimate customers a face, so you are no longer creating something for an anonymous nobody.

————

The phrase "sign-off" doesn't have to be figurative. You can literally sign your name to the products and services you create—even if you only leave the signature on your desk. If you're not proud enough to sign off on it, your boss probably doesn't want it shipped either.

STRATEGY

Business strategy is divided into *two parts. The first is the ability to see ahead. Good chess players look at the board with the future in mind. They consider what the effect of each move will be much later in the game.*

*T*he second part of business strategy is the ability to *see opportunities*. In the words of Trout and Reis, the authors of the classic *Positioning*, "find a hole and fill it."

Back in 1978, the average person might have looked at supermarket shelves and just seen rows and rows of bottles filled with natural juices. Gordon Crane saw a juicy opportunity. He challenged the market leader, Ocean Spray, by introducing the first apple-cranberry juice sweetened only with apple juice. He didn't stop there. Analyzing national orange juice sales, he discovered that "refrigerated orange juice in cartons was the number-one selling juice, with apple juice in glass containers the runner-up. I thought, why not marry the two best-selling package forms and introduce apple juice in a carton that can be sold in dairy sections?" In 1982, Crane's company, Apple and Eve, launched its new "brik-pak" juice boxes. Now when the average person looks at supermarket shelves, guess what she sees? Rows and rows of little boxes filled with natural juices.

Marcel Bich saw the opportunity to market a low cost, reliable, disposable pen. He outstrategized the competition by constantly inventing new products that would compete with his own pens—making it almost impossible for someone else to grab part of the market. Annual 1994 sales of the Bic company? $1.1 billion.

When Robert Siegel took over as chairman of Stride Rite Corporation at the end of 1993, he said, "No one was thinking of tomorrow." Products were losing money and sales were stagnant. The root of the problem was that Stride Rite was selling *products*, not *brands*. Siegel aimed to turn this around by opening special children's stores, launching new advertising campaigns, and repackaging and repositioning the Stride Rite brands, which include Keds sneakers and Sperry Topsiders. Said Siegel, "I love to build brands." And also: the man who was responsible for creating Dockers—a $1 billion brand for Levi Strauss—is clearly quite good at seeing the opportunities for brand-building.

Strategic is not always synonymous with conventional. Founders of the highly successful restaurant chain Outback applied some innovative management strategies which led to phenomenal growth and strength. Their idea: most chain restaurants have centralized management and the organizations aren't fast enough or flexible enough to do as well as they might. By giving each restaurant manager a piece of the profit pie and insisting that they invest in the restaurant, management created an entire new layer of owners. And owners, as everyone knows, mind the store better than anybody else.

When Reuben Mattus invented Häagen-Dazs in 1959, it wasn't just ice cream he was selling. Anyone can make good ice cream. The challenge was making people want his ice cream for a very specific reason. The niche in the market for superpremium ice cream was wide open, and he intended to fill it. But first, he needed to communicate the quality and mystique he had in mind. He positioned Häagen-Dazs as a foreign brand, complete with a map of Scandinavia on the package. Americans, who have an inferiority complex when it comes to taste and think anything European has to be better, gobbled up Häagen-Dazs, although it's made in New Jersey!

What you said about
STRATEGY

Organizational members need to have a sense for the strategic direction of the organization and how their actions support that direction.

DR. S. ROBERT HERNANDEZ
President, Healthy Industry Forum

Strategic—"Doing the right things is more important than doing things right."

JOSEPH STEMLER
CEO, La Jolla Pharmaceutical Co.

Strategic—It's important that everybody thinks strategically—things are changing too fast. We must be doing the right thing well.

PAUL BORDEAU
President, Bourdeau Consulting

TOWARD VIRTUOSITY

Strategy isn't just about big decisions. You use strategy when you choose a place for lunch with a big client. One way to develop your strategic thinking is to start with the small stuff and work your way up.

Try working backwards instead of from the beginning. Chess players think about the goal, then determine how to get there. When solving a problem, write down the end result you'd like to accomplish.

Play games of strategy. Checkers, chess, bridge, or poker, they all help develop your strategy. But fair warning: don't try this at the office.

If your speech is filled with words like respond and react instead of plan and predict, your actions will probably follow. Make your language strategic.

You can read a lot about strategy. Books on politics are filled with great examples of brilliant strategists. Try Lee Atwater or James Carville. Michael Porter wrote three classic books about business strategy. And more than one thousand years ago, Sun Tzu wrote a book called *The Art of War*—still relevant strategy today.

TEAMWORK

Kids play team sports: football, *baseball, soccer. Adults pursue solitary sports, such as swimming, running, and bowling. Do you see any connection to the difficulty some grownups have working in teams?*

*I*f emperor penguins in Antarctica don't work together, they die. Period. Thousands of male penguins huddle together, providing each other enough warmth to last through the most brutal subfreezing weather. They take turns walking around the outside of the huddle while those in the middle sleep. Teamwork means survival, and the selfish don't survive.

―――――

Frederick Shaltz Jr., president of Delta Land Surveying & Engineering Inc., is the epitome of the boss as team player. He has his twenty-three employees vote on everything from bonuses and tardiness penalties to choice of insurance and dress codes. Employees even banned smoking, although Shaltz is a smoker. Because everyone has a stake in the decisions, they're more likely to work together to make them work.

―――――

Three years ago, a Frito-Lay plant in Lubbock, Texas, introduced work teams and cut out numbers of middle managers. Teams of hourly workers such as Juanita Garcia now make key decisions. Garcia and the ten other members of her potato chip team are responsible for everything, from potato processing to equipment maintenance. Garcia's group, at the top of Frito's rankings for more than a year, also determines crew scheduling and even interviews potential employees—once the sole domain of management. The team concept "frightened" Garcia at first, but now provides her with a sense of pride in her accomplishments.

―――――

At the Sequent Computer Systems company, a sponsor is assigned to every new employee. The sponsor introduces the employee to others, rounding up office supplies, training the new hire on the e-mail system, and imparting various aspects of company culture. It takes a sponsor about thirty minutes a day to help his/her new co-workers, a cost that's tiny compared with the benefits to the company. "One of the main values of this company is teamwork," said Barbara Gaffney, vice president for human resources. "New employees work better if they know the other players."

Charles Garfield, the president of Performance Sciences Corporation, has a very succinct way of defining teamwork: "we" rather than "I."

Teamwork can happen beyond the boundaries of a single company or business. W. Edwards Deming loved to tell a story about his car breaking down. He called a local gas station to come tow it, but a tow truck from a competing gas station came to fix Deming's car. Turned out the two gas stations had decided to team up, and share one tow truck.

The Chief of Operations at Shearson Lehman Brothers explained that the accounting department has monthly deadlines that are very tough on everyone. So all the other departments pitch in for a day, going down to accounting until the deadline has been met. The amount of good will and teamwork this monthly gesture fosters is incalculable—but it definitely benefits the company.

What you said about
TEAMWORK

Teamwork was voted a most important virtue by a whopping 40 percent of survey respondents—not surprising considering the inherent interdependence of the business world. More startling is the number of executives from diverse businesses who feel teamwork is critical *especially* in their particular fields.

Heroes and Lone Rangers are dead ducks. The real power is in capturing and utilizing the talent of diverse players to meet the organization's fundamental goals.

PETER DiGIAMMARINO
Vice President, AMS

Without teamwork, the internal competitiveness and time pressures of CNN's twenty-four-hour operation would become a ticking time bomb.

BRIAN NELSON
Producer/Correspondent, CNN

Team orientation is critical in the "production" process of serving customers in a hotel environment; all associates must know both their internal and external customers and how each associate's role factors into the overall customer experience.

RAY SYLVESTER
Managing Director, Westin Hotels

Much of the work performed by the group is in "extended" teams—with customers, suppliers, and/or the parent company in the UK—hence good communications and respect for other viewpoints are essential.

ANDREW PICKARD
Vice President Engineering, Rolls-Royce Inc.

Teamwork defines the means through which ideas, plans and learnings are best formulated, explored, and refined. "Global Teamwork" is one of Colgate's three shared values.

BRIAN SMITH
Director Global HR Strategy, Colgate Palmolive

We are a 100-year-old commodity-based company in a super-competitive marketplace— without teamwork we cannot hope to survive.

RICHARD LINVILLE
Vice President Human Resources, Harriet & Henderson Yarns Inc.

TOWARD VIRTUOSITY

Everyone's willing to be part of a team as long as they get their own way. The hard part of teamwork is letting someone else take the lead, trusting them to do as good a job as you would. How comfortable are you with this surrender of autonomy?

Are there any successful teams in your company? If so, ask to sit in on a meeting. If not, what is there about your company culture that's preventing good teamwork?

———

Office games can create a team by bringing a group together in a spirit of fun and icebreaking. At one successful small company, a weekly game helps people get to know each other by trusting the others with previously private information. An employee posts an anonymous statement about him- or herself and everyone else has to guess who wrote it. For example, "When I was twelve, I was arrested for skipping school," or "I toured with a ballet troupe and met Baryshnikov."

———

Trying to please your boss is often an individual effort; trying to please customers or clients requires team effort. Ask yourself what you're trying to accomplish when you make work decisions. Is there someone else in the company who could make a difference in how well your project turns out?

———

Make a list of those you think of as part of your team at work. Now double the number of people. Every day ask one "new" team member one work-related question.

———

Let people fail. Then be there to catch them when they fall. In successful teams, fingers don't get pointed.

———

Try offering a sincere compliment to each of your team members on a regular basis. It's amazing how far a bit of appreciation goes in making people pull together.

VISION

Rather than playing short-term
*market hunches, Warren Buffett, generally
known as "the world's richest investor,"
finds companies that will profit in the
future, buys all or part of them, then lets
them grow. By following his vision,
Buffett has built one of the largest
fortunes in the United States.*

Vision is not the same thing as sight. And scientists now have proved it. Boston researchers demonstrated that the human eye has two distinct visual systems and one is completely independent of its ability to see. Jane Brody, in a *New York Times* article, wrote, "Just as the human ear controls both hearing and balance, the eye, these researchers showed, not only permits conscious vision but also registers light impulses that regulate the body's internal daily clock. Even people who are totally blind and have no perception of light can have normal hormonal responses to bright light."

"I skate to where the puck is going to be, not where it has been." Wayne Gretzky

---

Communicating a vision is as important as having one. Part of Ronald Reagan's success was his ability to convey his dream so effectively, using his performance skills.

In *21st Century Leadership*, Microsoft Chairman and CEO Bill Gates is quoted: "Our vision for Microsoft is, 'A personal computer on every desk in every home.' We have this constant direction and can see how everything fits. That broad, initial vision was written down when the company was started fifteen years ago and it has not changed. Many things have grown out of that, including the idea of having information at your fingertips. According to our vision, you should be able to bring up on a computer screen anything you are interested in. These are the visions we are striving to achieve."

The mission credo of Johnson & Johnson translates vision into practical daily guidelines. General Motors, under chief executive Roger Smith, placed a high value on getting the company's long-term vision shared by all employees.

"You must scale the mountain if you would view the plain." Chinese proverb

---

Roy Gaulke, COO of the Public Relations Society of America, said, "We don't teach people in school how to color outside the lines. We have to cultivate the attitude: how would we do it if there were absolutely no rules? When I worked for *USA Today*, it was the first four-color newspaper in America. Advertisers kept saying they didn't have any four-color material. So I suggested that we create a four-color advertising network and sell to newspapers other than *USA Today*. Everyone said, 'Are you crazy, sell ads to competing newspapers?' But Allen H. Neuharth was chairman of Gannett at the time. He saw the potential and it's now a huge successful advertising network."

"You can't win by comparing yourself to where you were last year. You've got to remember that the other guy is learning, too, so you actually have to go faster than the leader to catch up." Ralph Gomory, President, Alfred P. Sloan Foundation

What you said about
VISION

Without the vision to anticipate and adapt to change the most productive worker today will be unproductive tomorrow. Our company went from a "blue collar craft" to "high tech" in six years.

RICHARD TULLY
President, Pergda Industries

The ability to see beyond the walls of your business is vitally important to achieving greatness.

TAEGAN GODDAD
Project Manager, Office of Policy and Management

At an execut͏͏ individuals need to formulate and articulate where an organ͏͏ ͏͏ should be in the future. As the associates subscribe to the vision, all e͏͏͏͏ ͏͏ focused in the same direction.

ROD CHALLY
Director of Human Resources, National Merchandise Co.

It is imperative for companies to have leaders who can envision what the future will bring, describe how the organization will maximize its resources to fulfill its potential. This is the basis for all other components.

WILLIAM PALMER
Director, Duramed Pharmaceuticals

TOWARD VIRTUOSITY

Could you describe your company's vision? Is it the same vision *you* would choose for the organization?

———

The biggest vision "blinder" is the day-to-day crush of events. Set aside time to remove yourself from the daily hustle, to just think about the big picture.

———

Sometimes looking at a situation from a different perspective leads to visions beyond your wildest dreams. It's like an editor we know who used to proofread an entire magazine—upside down. He claimed that way he caught errors he would surely otherwise miss. Apply the upside-down technique to larger issues, and you might come up with a truly visionary approach.

———

Communicating your vision isn't easy. People are scared of intangibles. Are there simple analogies you can use to describe the picture you see of the future?

NOTES

Page

11   Rick Johnson, founder and CEO of BurJon Steel: Sara J. Noble, *301 Great Management Ideas*, Inc. Publishing, 1991.

11   When Benjamin Franklin tried to get printing work: Peter Hay, *Book of Business Anecdotes*, Facts on File, 1993.

12   It has long been an axiom of mine: Lewis D. Eigen and Jonathan P. Siegel, *The Manager's Book of Quotations*, Amacom, 1989.

12   An old hand at training seminars: John M. Capozzi, *Why Climb the Corporate Ladder When You Can Take the Elevator?*, Villard Books, 1994.

13   In *Quality Is Free*: Philip B. Crosby, *Quality Is Free*, McGraw-Hill, 1979.

16   John F. Raynolds III, the chairman and chief executive: Hal Lancaster, "Managing Your Career," *Wall Street Journal*, October 18, 1994.

20   According to Harvard Business School's John Kao: *Fortune*, January 10, 1994.

20   Russian immigrant Joseph Kaplan: *New York Times Magazine*, January 1, 1995.

21   I used to think that anyone doing anything weird was weird: Tom Peters, *Thriving on Chaos*, Knopf, 1987.

21   Robb Gaynor is a twenty-seven-year-old manager at Charles Schwab: Patricia Sellers, "How to Manage the Busters," *Fortune*, December 12, 1994.

22   The nine person wants to be a know-it-all: Eigen and Siegel, *The Manager's Book of Quotations*.

27   Sumner Redstone could have stopped being curious years ago: Robert Lenzner and Marla Matzer, "Late Bloomer," *Forbes*, October 17, 1994.

28   Twelve years ago, Delta Wire Company had ten employees: Jim Million, *Smart Workplace Practices*, December 1994.

28   We're not looking for any specific knowledge: Hal Lancaster, "Managing Your Career," *Wall Street Journal*, November 8, 1994.

28   John F. Raynolds III, chairman of Ward Howell International: Lancaster, "Managing Your Career."

29   Carol Caruthers said, "People don't remember your mistakes: Mary Rowland, "From the Gospel of Never Too Late," *New York Times*, January 1, 1995.

32   As star golfer Nancy Lopez once said: Michael Lynberg, *Winning!*, Doubleday, 1993.

32   Ella Williams started her own defense contracting firm in 1981: Wendy Dubit, "Try, Try Again," *Entrepreneur*, November 1993.

33   Alphonse Fletcher, the twenty-eight-year-old CEO and founder of Fletcher Asset: Sellers, "How to Manage the Busters."

36   One of IBM chairman and chief exec Louis V. Gerstner's main goals: Steve Lohr, "On the Road With Chairman Lou," *New York Times*, June 26, 1994.

36 Organizational consultant Harrison Owen developed the concept of "open-space": Claudia H. Deutsch, "Round-Table Meetings with No Agendas, No Table," *New York Times*, June 5, 1994.

37 I would I could stand on a busy corner, hat in hand: Eigen and Siegel, *The Manager's Book of Quotations*.

41 We've blown the whistle on some clients: Robin Dellabough, "On the Ropes," *Forecast*, November/December 1994.

41 It's not just whether it's legal or illegal; it's whether it's right or wrong: Capozzi, *Why Climb the Corporate Ladder...*

41 In a recent study, more than 80 percent of executives said: "How to Foster Honesty in Your Company," *Investors Business Daily*, December 5, 1994.

41 According to Malcolm Forbes Jr., Dial Corporation CEO John Teets: *Forbes*, November 21, 1994.

43 Company CEOs spend 90 percent of their lives making their companies look good: *Fortune*, October 17, 1994.

47 The story of Omar Aziz and his New Orleans Famous Omar Pies: Dubit, "Try, Try Again."

47 The chairman and CEO of IBM, Louis V. Gerstner, was quoted: Lohr, "On the Road With Chairman Lou."

48 Most people who come into Andersen spend the next ten years working: Sellers, "How to Manage the Busters."

48 No passion so effectually robs the mind of all its power of acting: Eigen and Siegel, *The Manager's Book of Quotations*.

53 Viacom chairman Sumner Redstone said, "Great successes: Lenzner and Matzer, "Late Bloomer."

57 To tend, unfailingly, unflinchingly, towards a goal: Eigen and Siegel, *The Manager's Book of Quotations*.

57 When Gordon Crane founded Apple and Eve juice company: Bob Weinstein, "Liquid Assets," *Entrepreneur*, October 1993.

58 A winner is someone who recognizes his God-given talents: Eigen and Siegel, *The Manager's Book of Quotations*.

58 And as William G. Dyer, of Brigham Young University: Eigen and Siegel, *The Manager's Book of Quotations*.

59 Too often people mistake being busy for achieving goals: *Harvard Business Review*, January/February 1987.

62 Some companies are trying to reduce employee stress on a day-to-day basis: *Wall Street Journal*, September 6, 1994.

62 The chief executive of Norand Corporation: Kate Bohner Lewis, "Listen, Learn and Sell," *Forbes*, September 12, 1994.

62 Never promise more than you can perform: Eigen and Siegel, *The Manager's Book of Quotations*.

63   When Jeffrey C. Barbakow took over as chairman of: Andrea Adelson, "The Job, Thankless; the Challenge, Huge. Let's Go," *New York Times*, July 31, 1994.

67   A young man began his career as a clerk in a department store: Hay, *Book of Business Anecdotes*.

67   Elected to the Baseball Hall of Fame in 1995: *New York Times*, January 10, 1995.

67   Working hard becomes a habit, a serious kind of fun: Lynberg, *Winning!*.

67   Jonathan Dolgen, chairman of Viacom Entertainment Group: Bernard Weinraub, "The New Man in a Hollywood Hot Seat," *New York Times*, July 24, 1994.

68   It takes five years of very hard work to become an instant success: Capozzi, *Why Climb the Corporate Ladder…*

68   I see myself as a doer. I'm sure that other people have had ideas: Roger Oech, *A Whack on the Side of the Head*, Warner, 1983.

68   Opportunities are usually disguised as hard work: Rowes, *The Book of Quotes*, Dutton, 1979.

72   When Ann Winkleman Brown took over the helm at the Consumer Product Safety: Brian Steinberg, "Adding Some Prime-Time Sizzle to Product Safety," *New York Times*, September 11, 1994.

72   In *The Seven Habits of Highly Effective People*: Stephen Covey, *The Seven Habits of Highly Effective People*, Simon & Schuster, 1989.

77   Honesty is the cornerstone of all success: Eigen and Siegel, *The Manager's Book of Quotations*.

77   Ignorance is not a simple lack of knowledge: Ryszard Kapuscinski, "The Philosopher as Glib Employer," *New York Times Magazine*, January 1, 1995.

83   A man should keep his mind with an attic stocked: Eigen and Siegel, *The Manager's Book of Quotations*.

83   Knowledge and human power are synonymous: Eigen and Siegel, *The Manager's Book of Quotations*.

88   Writer and scholar Warren G. Bennis once said: Eigen and Siegel, *The Manager's Book of Quotations*.

88   The number one leadership skill is the ability to develop others: Peters, *The Pursuit of Wow*.

88   We have to undo a 100-year-old concept: Alan Deutschman, *Fortune Cookies*, Random House, 1993.

89   Carol Caruthers, the national director of financial planning: Rowland, "From the Gospel of Never Too Late."

89   I cannot do what most of my employees can do: Eigen and Siegel, *The Manager's Book of Quotations*.

90   It is commitment, not authority, that produces results: Eigen and Siegel, *The Manager's Book of Quotations*.

90   A leader is a dealer in hope: Eigen and Siegel, *The Manager's Book of Quotations*.

90   In the book *21st Century Leadership*: Lynne Joy McFarland, Larry E. Senn, and John R. Childress, *21st Century Leadership*, Leadership Press, 1994.

94   An ounce of loyalty is worth a pound of cleverness: Eigen and Siegel, *The Manager's Book of Quotations.*

94   John Capozzi tells the following remarkable story of loyalty: Capozzi, *Why Climb the Corporate Ladder...*

95   In politics, loyalty is everything: Eigen and Siegel, *The Manager's Book of Quotations.*

95   The consummate Washington insider: *New York Times Magazine*, January 1, 1995.

96   The manager who supports the boss: Mary Ann Allison and Eric Allison, *Managing Up, Managing Down*, Simon & Schuster, 1984.

99   Ken Tuchman started out in business by importing: Jacqueline M. Graves, "He's pioneering a new industry," *Forbes*, December 12, 1994.

99   People can smell emotional commitment: Peters, *The Pursuit of Wow.*

99   Sunkist Growers, the orange cooperative: Peters, *The Pursuit of Wow.*

104   Rebecca Cole has built her business from being resourceful: Anne Raver, "One Person's Trash Is Another's Garden," *New York Times*, January 15, 1995.

109   Intel acted like Mr. Spock: John Markoff, "Intel's Crash Course on Consumers," *New York Times*, December 21, 1994.

109   Gordon Segal, founder of Crate and Barrel: *Profit*, November/December 1994.

110   In The *Joy of Working*, Denis Waitley and Reni Witt wrote: Denis Waitley and Reni L. Witt, *The Joy of Working*, Dodd, Mead & Company, 1985.

110   Nordstrom, home of legendary customer service: Jay Levinson, "Guerilla Selling," *Home Office Computing*, April 1994.

114   Ivan G. Seidenberg started at NYNEX right out of high school: Edmund L. Andrews, "A Ladder-Climber Reaches the Highest Rung at NYNEX," *New York Times*, November 29, 1994.

114   The day I started as a ticket agent I also started my own promotion plan: Capozzi, *Why Climb the Corporate Ladder...*

114   Maxwell Eaton started his own awning manufacturing company called Otter Creek: *Entrepreneur*, November 1993.

115   Let this be your motto—Rely on yourself: Eigen and Siegel, *The Manager's Book of Quotations.*

115   The American system of ours, call it Americanism: Eigen and Siegel, *The Manager's Book of Quotations.*

115   At age twenty-five, Didem Altop: Sellers, *How to Manage the Busters.*

118   The sales director of a large New York corporation hired a theater director: Hay, *Book of Business Anecdotes.*

119   Computer scientist Vinton Cerf is best known: Katie Hafner, "For Father of the Internet, New Goals, Same Energy," *New York Times*, September 25, 1994.

148

119 Ann Landers once said, "Don't accept your dog's admiration: Capozzi, *Why Climb the Corporate Ladder...*

119 What we are looking for first and foremost is a sense of humor: Peters, *The Pursuit of Wow.*

120 How much grief could be avoided if everyone at the workplace: Eigen and Siegel, *The Manager's Book of Quotations.*

124 Harry Quadracci started one of the largest printing companies: Daniel Kehrer, *Doing Business Boldly*, Random House, 1989.

124 For many years, France's Groupe Michelin held steadfastly: *Wall Street Journal*, September 2, 1994.

130 In the words of Trout and Reis: Al Ries and Jack Trout, *Positioning*, McGraw-Hill, 1981.

130 Back in 1978, the average person might have looked: Weinstein, "Liquid Assets."

130 Marcel Bich saw the opportunity to market a low cost, reliable, disposable pen: *New York Times*, January 1, 1995.

130 When Robert Siegel took over as chairman of Stride Rite Corporation: Zina Moukheiber, "They Want Mules, We'll Sell Mules," *Forbes*, September 12, 1994.

131 Strategic is not always synonymous with conventional: Jay Finegan, "Unconventional Wisdom," *Inc.*, December 1994.

135 Frederick Shaltz Jr., president of Delta Land Surveying & Engineering: Noble, *301 Great Management Ideas.*

135 Three years ago, a Frito-Lay plant in Lubbock, Texas: "Team Player: No More Same-ol-Same-ol," *Business Week*, October 17, 1994.

135 At the Sequent Computer Systems company a sponsor is assigned: Noble, *301 Great Management Ideas.*

136 Charles Garfield, the president of Performance Sciences Corporation: Eigen and Siegel, *The Manager's Book of Quotations.*

141 Vision is not the same thing as sight: Jane Brody, "Human Eye Found Doing Second Job," *New York Times*, January 5, 1995.

141 In *21st Century Leadership*, Microsoft chairman: McFarland, Senn, and Childress, *21st Century Leadership.*

142 You can't win by comparing yourself to where you were last year: Deutschman, *Fortune Cookies.*